GROWING PLACES

JAY KESLER

FLEMING H. REVELL COMPANY
OLD TAPPAN, NEW JERSEY

Library of Congress Cataloging in Publication Data

Kesler, Jay.
    Growing places.

    1. Youth—Religious life.   I. Title.
BV4531.2.K46   248'.83   77-26804
ISBN 0-8007-0904-7

TO the men who taught and encouraged me to face my world honestly, to grow into open relationships, and to take risks.

TO the men who preceded me in this office: Torrey Johnson, Robert A. Cook, Ted W. Engstrom, Carl J. Bihl, and Sam Wolgemuth. I appreciate their leadership under pressure more every day.

Contents

Preface

Throughout my life I have been surrounded by people, most of them young, searching, and emotionally intense. In Youth for Christ I have spent most of my time either speaking or counseling teenagers.

To survive such an environment, I've had to develop certain skills. Young audiences demand wit, honesty, and fresh ways of packaging the Gospel. I have to work—and it's exhausting, often frightening work—to hold the attention of restless audiences.

The environment of people has been a great place for me to work out a theology and a style. I get instant feedback on how well I'm communicating and whether God is using my style effectively.

There's one problem: those skills commit suicide when they're transcribed onto paper. The jokes aren't funny; the stories aren't detailed enough; the structure is too loose. Remember reading transcripts from the Watergate tapes in the newspaper? The conversations didn't make plain sense in newsprint. Inflections, body language, and emphasis were lost.

Most speakers get around this problem by hiring a ghostwriter, who does a quick edit job on verbal transcripts. But that's insufficient. The skills of a writer— research, sustained attention, emotional flow, shades of meaning—involve far more than a quick rewrite.

This book began with long hours of conversation by the beach in Florida, in a Texas hotel room, and in my backyard in Illinois. Then, Philip Yancey, the writer, read dozens of my sermons and speeches. After defining topic areas, he researched related books and articles and added his own

7

strong insights. Philip and I have a friendship, developed over many years, that is trusting and open.

The result is a true collaboration of two styles—the speaker's and the writer's. Because it came from dialogue and shared experience, we believe it truly expresses a blending of thoughts. Every word and paragraph came through the highly trained grid of Philip Yancey's mind. I am grateful to him.

JAY KESLER

Philip Yancey, editor of *Campus Life* magazine, has also written *After the Wedding: Nine Couples Tell How They Survived the Most Dangerous Years of Marriage* and *Where Is God When It Hurts?*

In my opinion whatever we may have to go through now is less than nothing compared with the magnificent future God has in store for us. The whole creation is on tiptoe to see the wonderful sight of the sons of God coming into their own . . . .

It is plain to anyone with eyes to see that at the present time all created life groans in a sort of universal travail. And it is plain, too, that we who have a foretaste of the Spirit are in a state of painful tension, while we wait for that redemption of our bodies which will mean that we have realized our full sonship in him.

Romans 8:18, 19; 22, 23 PHILLIPS

1

Bigger Boxes

It is when we notice the dirt that God is most present in us; it is the very sign of His presence.

C. S. LEWIS

The evening meeting of the Indiana Youth for Christ (YFC) camp was over. I stepped out into the moist breeze, ready for a quiet, unwinding walk along the shore of Winona Lake. It was good to be alone for a moment, away from the hundreds of squirming, noisy teenagers.

I slipped off the lighted sidewalks toward the path that circles the lake. Just as I turned my back on the buzzing conference center, I heard a voice, "Jay, Jay—is that you?"

I wanted to keep walking. I had talked to kids all day long, and I needed rest. But the voice had a certain urgency to it, and I responded. Three teenagers were waiting for me; two guys and a girl rushed to me and grabbed my arm. "Jay, you've got to come!" the girl said. "Cindy needs you—now!"

Together we went to see Cindy. What would I find—a drug overdose? Slashed wrists? An unwed mother?

Instead, I found a beautiful girl in blue jeans with her head bent down and long hair flowing over her knees. She was sitting cross-legged in a chair, sobbing, and as she cried, her body rocked back and forth.

I touched Cindy's arm, and she looked up with a pained

expression. She swallowed hard and began by saying, "Jay, I need help." We found a quiet corner away from the bustling lobby, and she opened up. "Jay, I need to know something. I'm almost besieged by Christians. My three friends who got you are Christians. My boyfriend's a Christian. My roommate at camp is a Christian. I'm surrounded!"

As I listened, Cindy visibly calmed. "But, Jay, I'm not a Christian at all. I've never wanted to be one before. Please, Jay, tell me the truth. I need your answer. Don't lie to me. I think some preachers have lied to me. Does this Christian thing really work? Does it *work?*"

She was quiet now, curled up against the wall waiting for my answers. Often I had jumped into situations like this with a quick "Of course it works. Christ is the answer." I sensed Cindy needed something more honest.

I considered Cindy's friends and what they might have told her about their faith. Possibly the image of the Christian life they had given her would not work. Some of the kids at camp described a honeymoon spiritual experience, full of joy and singing and void of pain. They wouldn't admit to doubts or struggles. I knew that Cindy could home in like radar on the weaknesses in their simplistic approach. Probably it was holding her back now.

Sitting in the shadows of the musty hotel hallway, hearing the soft breathing of this young girl, I thought, too, of my own experience. Could I be the answer man for her? Did it work for me?

I thought for a long time, then told her something like this: "Cindy, I just don't know. I want to say it will work for you, but I can't. In a sense, that depends on how you respond to Christ. You'll always have doubts and failures. All I can do is compare my life before I accepted Christ and after. A lot has remained the same. Some things have gotten even harder, more complex. But I have to tell you, my life with Christ has been infinitely more satisfying. Accepting Christ was the starting place. Choosing Him was like choosing a path to walk down—and I'm still plodding toward the destination.''

Cindy listened for an hour as I explained to her what Christ had meant to me. I'm not sure how our time together affected her. She thanked me and disappeared. But that hour with Cindy forced me to trace back through my past and follow the threads of my own spiritual experience.

These last twenty years, my job has squeezed me into some peculiar situations. Part of the week, I'm a normal businessman, working in an office setting of coffee breaks, telephone calls, lunch appointments, and daily calendars. But the rest of the time, I'm thrust, alone and defenseless, before the most overwhelming group of people I know—teenagers like Cindy.

This kind of life has affected me. Mainly, I guess, it's made me face myself and examine every claim I make about my faith. "Jay, do you really believe that?" I'm forced to ask about whatever I say. Teenagers may be immature and idealistic, but they've perfected one quality: the ability to spot hypocrisy. You can't slide weak logic or phony faith past them.

This constant pressure to reexamine and make sure is what made me decide to write this book. I've been forced to plunge headfirst into the tension areas of the Christian life. Teenagers won't let me gloss over problems with slick solutions.

Reality has shattered many of the preconceptions I had when I became a Christian. The brand of religion I practiced in high school has proved too small, and I've had to strip before God many times, asking to be taught all over again as His child. I would rather write a devotional book full of good answers and warm thoughts. But my Christian life has also included times of turmoil, when nagging problems pounded inside my head.

As I've shared my frustrations with Christian friends,

(*Drawing by Chas. Addams;* © *1974, The New Yorker Magazine, Inc.*)

invariably I have found them going through the same experiences. A whole breed of us was raised on the uniquely American proposition that there is a right answer to every problem. That formula hasn't worked for me. Oh, I've found guidance and strength and plenty of joy in my Christian life, but I have found them through a wholly different process than I thought I would. That's the key word—*process*. The Christian walk for me has been a series of flexes, bends, tremblings, and retracings.

I'm just now beginning to realize that perhaps that's the way it was meant to be!

For many years I looked at my faith as a series of boxes. When I became a Christian in high school, the box consisted of a rigid set of rules and pat answers. Who was a Christian? Anyone could spot one by noticing who didn't show up at the parties and who carried a red Bible on top of his books.

With college came a bigger box. I met a broader range of Christians, but the new limits of my behavior were still clearly defined. Progressing through each stage of life, I would trade in my box for a larger one. As I traveled, I took on a box that would meet approval both in Indiana and in Oregon. Then I expanded it to include overseas cultures. But always I saw the Christian life as a clearly defined set of rules. If I could just be consistent and keep all those rules, I would have it made.

That began to change. With amazement and not without a little fear, I began to see that there was no final corrugated tractor-trailer-sized box at the end of my Christian life. In fact, my whole concept had been faulty. Jesus seemed to dismantle my boxes one by one and say, "No, the life commitment to me is even harder than that. You can't put a lid on it. In fact, what I want from you is impossible."

Impossible? How can that be? Well, read the Sermon on the Mount. Jesus brings up the strict moral rules of the Jews and, one by one, devastates them. Adultery? "No," He says. "Anyone who even looks at a woman with lust in his eyes has already committed adultery with her in his heart." Love? That's not just for your friends, He says. "I say, love your *enemies!*" Murder? "I have added to that rule," Jesus says. "If you are only *angry,* even in your own home, you are in danger of judgment!"

With ideals like that, I feel very vulnerable and dependent. My life cannot be a sealed box. It has to be a continuous process of relying on God. I can never "arrive."

Bruce Larson uses this illustration: Have you ever been caught in a basement during a blackout? Imagine it. Suddenly everything is dark. You stumble around, banging boxes and table corners with your shins and thighs, fumbling awkwardly for some familiar object in the room. Then you reach a prized drawer full of every valued object you couldn't bear to discard. You rummage blindly through the shapes and sizes until you find a candle.

Soon that candle becomes your lifeline. Its flickering flame is the only source of light, and it casts a shadow on everything in the room. By it, you see your surroundings.

But just as you pick up the boxes and tools you've kicked aside and start toward the stairs, electric power surges, and the room is filled with light. Seconds before, the candle was your precious shaft of light to see the room. Now it's a puny pinpoint of flame, barely visible.

The growth of Christ's freedom in me has been like that. The flickers of truth which were my lifeline years ago have been overwhelmed by the brilliance of His way. Just when I think the Christian life has finally been illuminated, plainly and step by step, I stumble into a larger floodlighted room yet to be explored. I sense that same fresh freedom has swept through a lot of people in recent years. It makes me quite sad to meet someone who thinks he has it all together, all figured out, with his God in a box.

I identify with the expert on Moses' laws who came to Jesus "to test Jesus' orthodoxy," as it is described in Luke 10:25. When Jesus asked what Moses' laws said about how to get to heaven, the man came up with the perfect answer: ". . . love the Lord your God with all your heart, and with all your soul, and with all your strength, and with all your mind. And you must love your neighbor just as much as you love yourself" (Luke 10:27).

The man then wanted Jesus to get specific. "Who is my neighbor?" he asked, apparently wanting Jesus to limit his task for him so he could get to work loving just the right people and no one else. Jesus replied with one of the best-known stories of the Bible—that of the Good Samaritan. I recently found something in the story I had overlooked. Jesus never answered the man's question. He never listed groups of people the man should love. He completely side-stepped the question and instead answered an entirely different question: Not "From what groups should my neighbors be comprised?" but "What does it mean for *me* to be a neighbor to all people?"

Jesus refused to define minimum requirements. He threw

the responsibility squarely back on the man. Instead of finding a group of neighbors to love, the man had to be a neighbor to anyone he passed by, even a stranger in a ditch. Ours is an impossible task. I can never say, "I have been a neighbor, in all situations, to all people." Jesus ripped apart my box and replaced it with a mind-blowing, open-ended command I can never fulfill.

I had always glorified the goal of "arriving" at the true Christian life. Conveniently, I usually defined what arriving should be in terms of attainable goals: obeying rules, witnessing, achieving *do*able things. But Jesus specialized in wiping out all those legalistic obligations, saying, "No, there's much more than that." He never replaced my goals with something easier; He replaced them with something impossible.

In a sense, the ideal Christian life is unreachable in the terms Jesus laid out. Only He is sinless. Yet we tend to do everything we can to make it attainable, by lowering our sights. Jesus gave me a model. He laid out explosive ideals, and He gave a source for strength. But He left me to work out the details on how I, Jay Kesler, in twentieth-century America would respond to the challenge.

Discovering this was frightening and awesome. The sense of "Well, I've almost made it" vanished forever. At any point from then on, I realized I was just a humble beginner. I had taken just a few bites, and Jesus was saying to me that I would never be fat. The life He offered me was open-ended.

My faith is a rugged, tumbling clash of tension and peace, joy and sadness, victory and defeat. Like a baby, I'm learning to walk in it and accept it as the place God meant for me to live out His commands. This is an account of what I've run up against in trying to do that.

2

Beginning

*When someone becomes a Christian he becomes a
brand new person inside . . . .*

2 Corinthians 5:17

My conversion to Christ came during my high-school
years. America was sailing in a calm, prosperous period,
and protest was far from our minds. We were fighting a war
in Korea, but the country seemed mostly oblivious to it. We
assumed victory was just a matter of time, since America
won all her wars.

Friends would sign phrases such as "See you on
Porkchop Hill" in my yearbook. But despite the vague
threat of dying, we were carefree and apathetic. The working class, including my family, had taken a quantum leap in
prosperity since World War II, and we were bent on enjoying it.

Dating, fraternities, letter jackets, crew cuts, and making
out were the status symbols of my high school. There were
two groups—hoods and good kids. The hoods, wearing cig-
arette packs rolled up in their shirt sleeves, hung around the
drive-in and the town's gas station. Along with most of the
good kids, I worked hard at being popular and accepted.
My prime goal was to be liked by everybody. I even spent
time with the losers of the school. My father had instilled in
me a strong appreciation for the downtrodden; so I often
went out of my way to befriend those kids who were usually
ignored.

Phyllis was one of the few who managed to survive the
pressure to belong to one of the accepted groups. She was

not the most popular girl in school, didn't follow the latest styles, and rarely dated. But unlike other kids who felt in the "out group," she didn't slink through the halls with her head down, brushing against the lockers. She always looked right at me and smiled whenever she saw me, or anyone else. She was so serene and peaceful that instead of seeming out of it, she made me feel I was missing something. Phyllis, you see, was a Christian—the first I'd encountered my own age.

I had little sympathy for religion. I saw it as a supportive crutch for the losers of the world who might never make it without help. Most of the outspoken Christians I knew went to a basement church that managed to have "annual revivals" at least three times a year. They clung together like a school of fish.

Everyone in school knew about Phyllis's beliefs. She carried a Bible on top of her books and would read it at her desk before class, amid the clanking sounds of slammed lockers and noisy hallways. I think she was enticing someone to ask, "Why are you reading *that?*" Woe to the uninitiate who asked such a question. He immediately landed on Phyllis's target list, sure to receive a thorough explanation of her personal beliefs.

Once in speech class, Phyllis gave her testimony. It was alien to us. She used phrases such as "being born again" and "the Holy Spirit." While she was speaking, her head was down, and she was tearing a piece of paper behind the lectern. I looked around at my friends, and we smiled knowingly, understanding how nervous it must make the poor girl to try to convert such an indifferent bunch. We didn't make faces or throw erasers. We just listened with a superior, yet tolerant, air. At the end of her speech, Phyllis looked up with a smile and held up her paper. It had been torn in the shape of a cross. She had trapped me in sympathetic pity and then had driven her point home.

Though they were not in our "in group," Phyllis and her

friends were kind and consistent and that attracted me. One day I was with a group of friends in the lunchroom. Those of us who were cool usually ate with a favorite teacher and exchanged general school gossip and a few ribald jokes. Our table included all the "in group" kids who tend to run every high school. We laughed the loudest and appeared to be the most confident kids in the lunchroom.

While we were eating, the teacher pointed his fork at Phyllis and her friends, who were saying grace. The Christians—eyes closed, quiet, reverent—seemed out of context in this atmosphere. Speaking loudly, the teacher said, "Why do those kids pray before they eat? Seems like they could leave their religion at church. School isn't the place for that."

Everyone nodded agreement in unison. But I felt a sudden desire to stand up for the underdog; so I said, "If you believe something, you ought to believe it all the time, don't you think?"

Surprised, the teacher challenged me. "Hey, Kesler, since you like them so much, why don't you join them?"

"I think maybe I will!" I retorted. Most of the guys knew I had to be joking.

I almost forgot that incident until a few days later when Phyllis stopped me in the hall. She had been inviting me regularly to the school Bible club.

As I talked to her, my embarrassment about the lunchroom incident flooded back. My words spoken in haste had contained truth. What right did we have to taunt the Christians of our school? Phyllis would never laugh at anyone cruelly. So, to Phyllis's delight, I agreed to go to the Bible club for the first time.

That lunch hour, I found myself listening to a visiting speaker talk on John 3:16. Though the Bible verse described love and forgiveness, most of his emphasis was on sin, and I felt self-conscious about mine. I caught a few kids sneaking looks my way to see how I was reacting. I listened nervously and mainly noticed little things about the speaker, such as his thick wrists. I had thought all Christians were effeminate, but this man certainly wasn't.

Inevitably, Phyllis stopped me in the hall the next day. "What did you think?" she asked with an eager smile.

"I thought it was unfair to talk about sinners when I was the only one there," I said. Phyllis told me how everyone had sinned, even her. She told me about a series of verses in Romans and asked me to come with her to a private place on the school stage. I was confused, but also more than a little concerned. If Phyllis was a sinner, where did that leave me?

In the next few minutes, Phyllis talked me into saying a prayer. I had started out being nice to this one Christian girl. Somehow, she had cornered me. The Christian idea sounded attractive, though I had no idea what it would later entail. I edged over to the curtain, and surrounded by dissonant band music, I prayed my first sincere prayer to God. It had no real content. I simply said yes instead of no to Him for the first time, asked Christ to forgive my sins, and quietly entered His Kingdom.

Phyllis was ecstatic. Moist eyed, she offered me a New Testament and asked me to meet with the Bible group in front of the school that next noon hour.

The noon meeting was my first exposure to what would be expected of me as a Christian. The Christians pushed a piano onto the front steps and sang songs such as "Do, Lord" with great enthusiasm. I sat near the back with a few friends—most were just killing time before classes and had come out of curiosity.

Suddenly Phyllis was standing up, talking. I could barely hear her, ". . . one of the fellows you all know. He's a Student Council officer, and he's just accepted Christ into his heart. I'm sure he'd like to tell you about it. Jay? . . ."

This I hadn't expected. Pulse racing, I shuffled to the front, bewildered. I fumbled around, trying to ignore my

"Well, whatever it is we change into, it can't come soon enough for me." (*Drawing by D. Reilly;* © *1973, The New Yorker Magazine, Inc.*)

friends in the back making wisecracks. I mumbled something about how I didn't want to be a hypocrite and I needed everyone's help, and then sat down. I was quite sincere, though I didn't understand much. The guys thought it was funny. They believed I'd engineered the event as a practical joke on the Christians.

But my life changed. That "accidental" lunchtime prayer, and my own Bible studies which followed it, set off a revolution inside me. I saw how much of my friendliness had been motivated by envy and greed—a desire to be popular. In fact, everything in my life had revolved around my own self-interest. In the Bible and through the Christian kids, I learned about self-giving.

Some of the changes were good. Others I wondered about, but they appeared to come with the Christian tag. I dived into the Christian life with unusual eagerness, totally unaware of the twists and pitfalls which lay before me.

3

Visible Symbols

*Christianity is not a state at which one arrives; it is a
life in which one matures.*

KEITH MILLER

One thing made Jesus most angry, and it was the first
trend I encountered as a Christian. It reached out and put a
viselike grip on me I'm still trying to shake.

Christ had revolutionized my life. My faith had infused
me with fresh joy and motivation, and I eagerly sought how
to become the best Christian who had ever lived. Soon I
found myself pulled into a new group, with strong pressure
to break all ties with my old friends. I learned all the new
rules which would be required of me. I could no longer
dance at the school proms I chaired. I couldn't smoke,
swear, tell dirty jokes, or go to movies. I was expected to
carry a Bible around. I couldn't get mad. I had to learn a
new Christian lingo and smile more often. Along with the
internal changes had come a complete set of dozens of rigid
externals. Every few days one of my new Christian friends
would point out a moral code I didn't know about.

By the end of that school year, I had lost my best friends
and been tagged with an entirely new set of people. If you
had asked my old set of friends what Christianity is, they
would have said, "Oh, that's what made my friend Jay
weird."

Soon I started causing tension in my family. My parents
were concerned that I was becoming a religious fanatic.

Before, I had always respected my Dad for his integrity and compassion, but within months of my conversion, I had branded him as a lost soul. All my friends who were conservative theologically were also conservative politically; so I rejected Dad for his liberal political views. Sadly, I saw these chasms which divided our family as badges of success. This was suffering for the Lord, I thought. Eventually, we just stopped talking about it.

When I went away to college that fall, the complexion of our family had changed. I had opened up sores among us. My father sat in the car with me one last time before I left. I'm sure he felt rejected by my superior attitude, and he hadn't bared himself to me in a long time. He took a deep breath. "Jay, what's with this religion?" he asked. "You were a balanced, healthy kid who loved life and music and had dates every weekend. Now you act like we're all evil and headed for hell and only you and a few friends are living right. If Christianity has any truth at all, there's more to it than your approach admits."

My Dad had nailed it. We weren't content to let Christ's love and the Holy Spirit guide us to become unique persons for Him. Instead we had manufactured a "Christian personality" mold that everyone had to be poured into. My life had truly changed, and I knew that Christ was my Saviour, but somehow I had become caught in a set of external rules and regulations. To me, Christianity included a straitjacket of pious legalism to wear the rest of my life.

And that's what made Jesus angry at the Pharisees. The Pharisees were the fundamentalists of their day—the orthodox, spiritual people. They followed Moses, just as the law prescribed. They were not bad people—just exclusive. And they cut others out with a cookie cutter, the shape of their own prejudice. They took pride in it, constructing a set of rules which set them apart from other people.

Even today, I fight the very same trend in myself. It's not so much rules now—I tend to get self-righteous toward people who don't have as much insight as I have or who aren't as open in sharing themselves or who are less committed than I am. But it's the same pride in different forms.

Teenagers, too, are still battling the issue with different forms. Instead of carrying a red Bible with schoolbooks, now it's wearing a Jesus sweatshirt or saying, "Praise God!" or blindly following some Christian speaker. A major emphasis is still on *visible symbols* of the faith. Too many kids haven't learned that changes are supposed to happen inside. They insist on being frontal, on fighting the battle on a surface level. As a result, they'll reject all their old friends and perhaps their parents, just as I did. Christianity becomes almost a uniform, existing mainly to declare what I'm not. I'm not a dancer, a cardplayer, a joke teller. But what am I? Am I giving the world a positive alternative?

The stifling effect legalism has had on me convinces me why Jesus struck against it so hard. Read Matthew 23. The strongest words Jesus ever used, He reserved for the most pious, moralistic people around Him.

Where do these oppressive ideas come from? In me, the trend to legalism stems from the inherent pressure to make the Christian life "arrivable." I *can* make it. I *can* succeed 100 percent as a Christian—that is, as long as I'm the one who defines what a Christian is. I then take that marvelously all-encompassing verse "Deny yourself, take up your cross, and follow me," and try to fill in the blanks. I replace it with "Deny something" and proceed to describe that something.

It would appear that two thousand years of Christian history would teach us the dangers. But still, every group has its own set of extrabiblical mores and "don'ts." I suppose I first started questioning the idea of legalism when I began traveling. Everywhere I went, groups felt intense moral pride about their own visible symbols. In South Africa, for instance, a good friend of mine was severely criticized. His sin? He chewed gum in public and prayed with his hands in his pockets! Elders took me aside and warned me about my

"Also in all times and in all places to condemn war, pollution, and non-biodegradable containers, to support the Third World, and to fight for a better life for the migrant farm worker." (*From William Hamilton,* Anti-Social Register. *Published by Chronicle Books,* © *1974.*)

friend's errors. (However, some of these same church leaders had difficulty seeing the evil in apartheid racial policies.)

Once again, a teenager made me face the problem square on. I was in a camp in Alabama in the early sixties—one of my first trips into the deep South before civil-rights victories. At first the use of the word *nigger* and the caricatured racial illustrations inflamed me. But I had come to bless these Christians, not offend them, I rationalized. After a few days I began feeling at home. As long as we stuck to the Gospel and didn't bring in these fringe issues and "social Gospel" everything was okay. These people may have been racists, but I'd never met a more warm, polite bunch of kids. They were clean-cut, committed, and they used the same Christian words I used. They listened attentively to what I said and nodded vigorously.

By the end of the week, I was complacent and satisfied. Then I talked to Richard. He followed me out after a meeting and stopped me. The summer night was warm and sultry, and we sat by the lake slapping mosquitoes and listening to the frogs croak. I thought he'd come to have me counsel him and straighten out his life. I was wrong.

"I could never receive your kind of God," Richard began. "Your God is trivial. He doesn't care about war, poverty, starvation, racism. He only cares about whether people smoke, drink, dance, go to the show, or make out."

Richard stunned me. Actually, I hadn't said anything about these things, but my silence on the larger issues had misled him. I thought through my own life. I had programmed all the right Christian behavior. I did all the right do's and avoided the wrong don'ts. Was my concept of God trivial? I began to see that it was. I had used the visible symbols—which had established me as a star Christian—as a cop-out, and I had ignored the real issues of love, integrity, and compassion which God has commanded.

I left the South burdened and heavy. Their brand of religion was no different from my own hypocrisy. I couldn't hide behind my Northerner's detached superiority. I, too, used Christ and my carefully devised set of petty rules as an escape. Did I even know the real Christ? Christ the Lion, Christ the Prophet, Christ the King? My Christ was a malleable, don't-talk-back support—little more. Had I truly listened to Christ's voice, or did I simply squeeze His message into my mold?

I had time off the next week, and while home in Indiana, I did some hard thinking. I thought back over the stages of my life. My growth as a Christian often meant taking on more and more rules. As I walked around in the backyard, I noticed my collie, Laddy. He was merrily gnawing on a bone, stretched out in the glistening wet grass. It struck me that Laddy was quite possibly the best Christian I knew, according to my terms. He didn't smoke, drink, go to shows, dance, or wear protest signs. He was harmless, docile, and inactive. That's how I had defined a Christian! Issues such as poverty, racism, hatred, lying—I considered them peripheral, because I'd found them so hard to deal with, and, besides, they weren't on my list.

Throughout the years since, I've done a lot of thinking about the topic of the visible symbols of our faith. There's a danger, of course, in overreacting to legalism and therefore abusing Christian liberty. The Bible is very explicit about certain behavior. Yet, throughout the centuries, Christians have wanted to add to the Bible's lists.

I've come to believe that rejecting legalism is the first step in accepting the idea of *process*. Legalism fights against process. It tempts us to say, "You've got the Christian life figured out. Just follow the rules and relax. There's nothing more to grow into."

It once puzzled me to read Christ's radical statements, such as, ". . . be perfect, even as your Father in heaven is perfect" (Matthew 5:48) and "One must renounce all he has to be a disciple" (*see* Luke 14:33). How could I ever literally fulfill those commands and dozens more just as radical?

I've begun to see, though, that Jesus taught to give direction rather than directions. He described the *goal* of good living. In this respect Jesus stood out in sharp contrast against the Pharisees, who sought to find specific rules every faithful Jew could follow.

By stating the loftiest ethical demands, with no apparent compensation for human nature, Jesus drives us to the idea of process—and to Himself. His love undergirds us as we grow in the Christian life. If we are truly His disciples, we will never stop growing. Next year I want to be a larger, deeper Christian than this year. I never will reach the point where I can say, "Well, I'm doing it. I'm living the Christian life as it was meant to be lived." But I can say, "God is teaching me to walk forward in victory, depending on Him for growth and guidance.

It helped me to think through the problem and list four dangers of legalism which stunted my growth as a Christian. Rather than dwelling on the negative, I want to state these dangers as positive alternatives to legalism.

Learn Principles, Not Dictums

Karl Olsson of Faith at Work, a Christian group committed to personal renewal, has helped me understand how we tend to turn the Bible's principles into dictums. Jesus turned them back around. He took the Pharisees' dictums and pointed to the principle. For example, people in Jesus' day had taken the command to honor the Sabbath and made that command a dictum. People couldn't even feed themselves or take care of a wounded animal on the Sabbath. Jesus set it in right perspective without destroying the principle of setting aside a day to focus on the Creator.

Our dictums may spring from truisms that have nothing to do with Christianity. For example, Olsson says he was taught the dictums, "Men don't express emotion" and "Sex is dirty." Others learn things such as "Christians don't get angry" and "Marriages shouldn't have conflicts." These are ghosts in the attics of our subconscious that enslave us. We lose freedom by being bound to these codes, which may or may not have a Christian base.

I have to turn to the Sermon on the Mount whenever I feel the trend toward dictums. Jesus goes right through the list of dictums of His day and explodes them. Notice He doesn't destroy the law. He shows us its true anchor—a desire to please God. He shows that we're all hypocrites, that we can't make it 100 percent as Christians, but we can follow Him.

A very tragic person taught me the horror of concretizing a principle of Scripture. This example is the most extreme I know of legalism and foolish literalism, and it shows how we can miss the point entirely. This Christian took even the Sermon on the Mount—the chief source of antidictums in the Bible—and hardened it unmercifully.

I was at a youth meeting in a barn in rural New Mexico. Most of the event had been taken up with games, except for a sermonette I delivered. After I finished, I was helping to clean up the straw and apple cores and paper cups when a girl approached me and referred to something I'd said in my talk.

"But I can never be a Christian," she blurted out. I looked up and saw that her eyebrows were fallen, and I could see fear and bitterness in her eyes.

I said as gently as I could, "Want to tell me why not?"

"Because it makes you crazy," she said, and her voice took on a hard edge. I just stood there, waiting. "Have you ever seen my dad, Jay?"

I told her, no, I'd never met him. "Well, when you see him, you'll know," she said and slipped off into the darkness.

Soon after that the young girl's dad came to pick her up. The car was full of giggling girls, but she made him get out and come over to meet me. While we exchanged a few pleasantries, I noticed nothing unusual about this man— nothing that would make his daughter lash out at Christianity so vehemently. He started back toward the car, but his daughter lingered on and said to me, "Do you know what I mean?" I didn't.

The girl then asked me if I'd seen her dad's foot. I had noticed it was severed below the ankle. "Now wait a minute," I began. "You're not going to hold that against him . . . ."

She stopped me short. "You believe the Bible, Jay. Well, so does my dad. He read that if your foot offends you, cut it off. So, one day he went out behind the barn, put his foot down on a chunk of wood, raised the ax, and cut it off. I don't want that kind of religion!" She was crying, and before I could even speak, she ran to her car and left.

This man had a sincere desire to please his God, but I'm with his daughter—I don't want that kind of religion either.

Raise Your Sights

When I was caught up in legalism, I felt proud almost all the time. I followed the rules; I had succeeded as a Christian. Some people think it's a lot harder to live a disciplined, straitjacket life. If you approach it the way I did, thinking I was serving God, it's actually easier. I had God all pegged in my box. Afraid to confront my own hypocrisy, I had set up a synthetic standard that I could meet. This way, I didn't have to fail.

By doing so, of course, I had lowered my view of God. I defined Him as the one who ruled my life. Actually my life was ruled by a narrow list of twentieth-century American mores to which I attached God. God is bigger than that.

I love the title of J. B. Phillips's book *Your God Is Too Small.* I think one reason more people are not Christians is because they look at the image of God we present to the world and see how small He is. In this way, our legalism is a block against the world. Like the boy I talked to in Alabama, people know the real issues are not clothes and hairstyles. They know a lot of Christians are missing what counts in life.

C. S. Lewis captures this concept of an ever-bigger God in an allegory from his Narnia series—*Prince Caspian.* Lucy, a young girl in a strange land, comes across Aslan, a huge lion who is a Christ figure.

> The great beast rolled over on his side so that Lucy fell, half sitting and half lying between his front paws. He bent forward and touched her nose with his tongue. His warm breath came all round her. She gazed up into the large, wise face.
>
> "Welcome, child," he said.
>
> "Aslan," said Lucy, "you're bigger."
>
> "That is because you are older, little one," answered he.
>
> "Not because you are?"
>
> "I am not. But every year you grow, you will find me bigger."

Work on the Inside Core

There are two parts to being a Christian: the inner core of worship and faith, and the outer results of that core, as seen in your actions. I've found it much easier to work on the outer effects. I can work on habits and patterns of action that get me accepted in most any group. But to tap into that slippery, intangible Source—that's work.

Whatever the expression "Christ living in you" means, I think it touches upon something here. Most of our beliefs, hobbies, and practices are improved by feeding them. We exercise. To become a tennis player, you get up in the morning, slap balls against a backboard for hours, do push-ups to strengthen your arm, and watch the pros' strategies on TV. To succeed in the stock market, you read everything written on it, pore over the *Wall Street Journal,* and talk to brokers.

Being a Christian does involve some exercises. But mainly, it involves a conscious growth in being aware of God's presence. That comes not through exercising, but through getting to know the Christ of Scripture as you would know a good friend. He Himself is a Source we can lean on for strength and guidance. We don't have to keep pumping Him up to stay excited about Him. Instead we need to learn to rest in Him.

In my work with teenagers and their parents, I've talked to hundreds of kids who grew up in wonderful Christian homes and in sound churches but decided later to junk their faith. They had been outstanding examples of Christianity—for a while. What went wrong?

I've come to believe that many of them failed by concentrating on the exterior. Their friends behaved a certain way and spoke a certain language, so they picked it up. They became walking mirrors, reflecting all the correct styles and patterns of the church. But inside, they were withered. Making faith an external exercise like that does something very risky—it makes faith easy to shed, like taking off a shirt. To discard this brand of Christianity, all you have to do is pick up a different set of rules and a new set of friends.

If you develop Christian strength by focusing your attention on the living Christ, though, it becomes much more difficult to shed. I know; I've tried. Once He's gotten a grasp on my life, and done miracles in me, I can't deny Him. He becomes a living presence.

If I had to draw a picture of what I wanted my Christian life to look like, I think I'd borrow one from Creation—the sunflower. One day I came across a sketch of a sunflower in a very technical magazine. The drawings in the magazine were illustrating a complex engineering principle. Every sunflower demonstrates the exact same arrangement of seeds; there are always fifty-eight rows. Each row starts in the center, close together, and builds in a widening spiral toward the outside. Because the center rows are so close, the sunflower bulges in the middle. This article described the concept and then applied it to dome building. Engineers have discovered that the sunflower-seed design is perhaps the strongest possible support design for a large dome. The sunflower picks up enormous support in the center, allowing the spirals to range far away without weakening the design.

I like that picture. I want my Christian life to be immovably, incredibly strong in the center core—the bedrock of my faith, where I put all my trust in Christ. By doing that, I gain strength to explore in adventurous areas. Like Jesus, I can have raucous non-Christian friends who are not a threat to my faith. I don't have to surround myself with comfortable, like-minded people. I can be in the world but not of it.

Legalism is a peculiarly subtle danger. It can give you all the same feelings which God's grace gives you: a lack of guilt, a sense of completeness, a confident strength. But there's one critical difference: <u>with legalism, I take the credit, not God</u>.

In his *Letters to an American Lady*, C. S. Lewis said, "Nothing gives a more spuriously good conscience than keeping rules, even if there has been a total absence of all real charity and faith." Very few of my outward symbols have changed since those early days. I don't smoke, drink, or dance for various reasons. But I have become convinced, *really* convinced, that those visible symbols have nothing to do with whether I get to heaven or not. That is up to God.

4

Rediscovering Grace

Christianity is strange. It bids man recognize that he is vile, even abominable, and bids him desire to be like God. Without such a counterpoise, this dignity would make him horribly vain, or this humiliation would make him terribly abject.

BLAISE PASCAL

I was lying facedown on a mattress—the only real piece of furniture I owned after three years of marriage. I listened to Janie preparing dinner in the kitchen that steamy August day in Indiana.

I thought back over the years of our romance. We had our courtship at Taylor University, a Christian college in rural Indiana. I had transferred there from Ball State University, because I felt God was calling me into the ministry. Taylor fit me fine—a perfect environment to exercise my spiritual muscles.

I had arrived at Taylor in a '49 Studebaker which I had

dedicated to the Lord. Inside it was a radio I had also dedicated, vowing to listen only to news or religious programs—no music. Every morning at 5:30 I would jump out of bed, hit the cold floor with bare feet, and begin reading my daily quota of twenty Bible chapters.

I especially loved the passage in which Paul lists his spiritual credentials (*see* 2 Corinthians 11:23). "Where some did this, I did much more," he had said, and I sprang to the challenge, determined to outdo Paul. I started preaching at nearby churches every night. In the wee hours of morning, when the campus was dark and still, my Studebaker would come wheezing in. In a few hours I'd be up again, attending classes, arguing theology, encouraging others to greater piety.

After a while, private devotions were not enough. I formed a group patterned after John Wesley's Holy Club which met under the organ pipes in a hole of the chapel basement. We faithful ones would attend every morning, huddled together, shivering in the dark like Christians in the catacombs.

This fierce dedication burned brightly, continuing after I met and married Janie. I worked at being more intense each year—getting up earlier, going to bed later, witnessing more boldly.

I remembered those days as I lay on the bed, in pools of my own sweat. I thought back over my "ministry." It had started with informal acts like sidling up to a bartender late at night and asking him if I could give my testimony and hand out tracts in his tavern. Soon I hit the local preaching circuit. As a student, I held 152 weeks of revival services in four years.

When Janie and I were graduated and married, I upped that to 360 nights of preaching a year. But what did I have to show for it in my young family?

We went through dinner that night quietly, without the usual chatter. I looked around at our home. A mattress on a

"It finally happened! The consumer price index is listing the cost of salvation." (*Reprinted with permission from* The Saturday Evening Post, © *1977.*)

frame. A TV set donated by some guys in the Taylor dorm. That was it: a bed, an old TV, and a battered Studebaker in the yard. For 360 nights of preaching, I had eked out $150 a month. But where was the warm glow of satisfaction I was supposed to feel?

My life-style didn't change that night. I kept on preaching, grinding it out. But something clicked in my mind. I had a moment of doubt. Was I going about "my ministry" all wrong? Was I trying too hard to do it *myself?*

Small grains of cynicism crept in. Why didn't I feel right? How did God fit into all my efforts?

Years of hurting and scrambling and warring passed before I was ready to stumble across a concept. It had been lacking from my Christian life from the beginning, and that lack had been at the root of my tendency toward legalism and the frenetic race toward superspirituality. It was the novel, awesome concept of grace.

There is something very unattractive about grace. We can focus easily on denying self, on tangible things other men can measure and praise us for. Grace is hard to swallow. It takes the credit off us and puts it on Christ. I had much preferred to take on false pain, mimicking martyrs, rather than giving God the glory.

Not until I began to sense my own inadequacies did I realize that I had been serving a distorted God. My picture of Him was harsh and demanding. To placate Him, I would rail about sin and preach harsh, judgmental sermons. Inside, though, I was filled with self-doubt and a desire to "out-orthodox" the most committed. Something drove me to prove myself to Him, over and over, earning respect, as it were.

Even when I failed Him, I would twist it around to prove my worth. I couldn't accept forgiveness handed to me freely because of the cross. I wanted to crawl on my belly, prostrate, proving my repentance. Perhaps more dedication and more separation from the world would make me more pleasing to God! How could I be pure and untainted?

Yet, as I discovered, there is no way to be completely pure in this world. When I buy gasoline, I may aid corporate bribery. If I buy an Arrow shirt or a Marantz stereo, I help pay for ads in impure magazines. I ride a Lockheed plane and help make nuclear weapons. In this kind of world, the only solution is grace. We sing about it, but I'm convinced most of us hate it when it means our efforts are not enough. We much prefer clinging to our pride.

Slowly, I learned the freedom of accepting my weaknesses. As a Christian, I had sought to impress others with how much better I was. Actually, the key difference between my outlook and the world's is that I admit to sin. I am guilty, but God has forgiven me, and all the credit is His. His love is not contingent on my performance. There is nothing I can do to make Him love me more.

Remember back in school, when grades were so important? After a test, some students would come up to others and ask, "How'd you do?" (Strange how the A students were the ones who usually asked!) If you got a C, you felt much more comfortable discussing the test with a fellow C student or a D student. You'd never approach an A student and talk over the problems you'd had. Sometimes I think we in the church give off the vibes of being A students. We've got it together; we've been redeemed; our sins have been forgiven. We want others to compare their D's and F's with our A's. No wonder non-Christians can feel strange around us!

I don't see those superiority vibes in the New Testament. I see men, like Paul, Peter, and John, who are humbly convinced of their shortcomings, and just as humbly rejoicing in God's grace. Through their weaknesses, He is made great. I read somewhere that Peter and John were the most rebuked of the twelve disciples. I looked through the Gospels and found it's true. Jesus continually turned on them for showing immaturity and selfishness. Yet he transformed them into His two most effective disciples.

I'm sure God used my frenetic efforts in those early days of my ministry. Some of the converts were converts to myself, but the Holy Spirit kept others and used me in spite of myself.

In addition, those years taught me something about process. I had already begun to learn how God's process operates in behavior. God had taught me His way was not a narrow, exclusive box. Now, He taught me that process applied to my ministry as well. The key in this area was to learn to trust Him. I shudder now, when I think back on how inadequate my view of God must have been during those years of striving. I couldn't trust Him. I had to personally handle every detail, even to the point of feeling personally responsible for results in evangelism, which should be the domain of the Holy Spirit.

If I had to summarize the first ten years of my ministry

with one word, I would choose *activity*. I was so busy *doing* that I had no time to learn to *be*. I learned that activity is not necessarily service. Americans, I think, are especially susceptible to the activity trap. TV and radio have attracted us to the quick and spectacular, and we see complex situations resolved in neat one-hour segments. In contrast, ancient man was forced by his society to move at a slower pace. Moses moved the children of Israel at the speed of the slowest lamb.

I began to see that much of my frustration as a leader sprang from my role as a performer, which led to sudden bursts of activity at a camp or conference. I often had only one-hour segments with an audience in which to challenge their faith. I never had three-month periods to share with them and show my life in process. By contrast, the apostle Paul wrote his epistles mainly as reminders to a church to recall what he had fleshed out among them.

What is it within us that makes us want to hurry up God, to accomplish His work in our own way at our own pell-mell pace? Helmut Thielicke, the German theologian, has expressed this drive as well as anyone I know. In his book *Encounter With Spurgeon* he says:

We hound our young vicars . . . chasing them from examinations into the bustling business of pastoral services in the big cities, from funerals to marriage, and from the pulpit to doorbell ringing, opening the pores of the body of Christ to all the bacilli against which, after all, we should be mobilizing the antibiotic of our message of peace. We keep killing flowers in the bud, because we are no longer capable of letting things grow. And we can no longer let things grow because down underneath we have forgotten how to pray "Thy kingdom come," and in its place have put our "manager's faith," our belief that everything can be produced and organized. We preach "Do not be anxious!"—and at the same time worry ourselves to death about whether everybody will hear this. We say, "God reigns"—and still we run about madly keeping the ecclesiastical machinery going. We proclaim man's passive righteousness (the righteousness that comes from God)—and still we behave like activists. We preach eternity; but when Jesus asks us, "Did you have enough of everything?" we will have to reply, "Oh, no, we didn't have enough time." This is why we preach peace and radiate restlessness. This is why we give stones instead of bread, and men do not believe us. The faith is refuted by the incredibility of those who proclaim it . . . .

The result of all this may be some kind of success, but it is not the fruit of the Spirit. It may be quite possible to register certain influences that the church has exerted upon public life, but they are not the salt that preserves from decay nor the leaven that determines the taste of the bread. The grain of wheat of the messenger and the grain of wheat of the church as institution must first be hidden in the earth, in quietness and calm passivity; it must first die if it is to be able to spring up and bear fruit. Yet we work feverishly, pushing things along with artificial fertilizers; we are perpetual "producers" worshipping the gods of production.

As a result of these discoveries, we in YFC began moving toward a discipleship ministry. Instead of relying solely on massive, one-shot rallies, we began yearlong series of club meetings in which a staff member would spend scores of hours with the same small group. We tried to model after Christ who wisely zeroed in on only twelve persons as the central core of His ministry. The staff began to proclaim the message of Christ on a relational basis.

Teenagers need a human model—one in whom they can

see the process of grace operating. They need to get close to a leader and see his struggles—and his victories. God was teaching me, through process, the way to become that model. It was to trust Him.

George Macdonald speaks to this point very clearly. "Foolish is the man," he says, "and there are many such men, who would rid himself of his fellows of discomfort by setting the world right, by waging war on the evils around him, while he neglects that integral part of the world where lies his business, his first business—namely, his own character and conduct."

Grace is two pronged, as Pascal noted in the chapter epigraph. As I relied on God for His strength and direction, I had to learn to be a servant. To serve God is not to impress Him with valiant efforts, as I had been trying. Am I serving a God who can be impressed?

Rather than being a servant, I had carved out a slice of work which fits my talents—speaking in front of kids—and constructed my life to further that goal. Elisabeth Elliot made the point in *No Graven Image* that God is not an accomplice to our work; He *is* the work. I needed to learn that.

I had envisioned the Christian life as being a supermarket counter, with various virtues laid out in an appealing row like shiny vegetables. Christians could pick and choose among them. Love was for people with easygoing personalities; courage for adventurers, and so on. As I had gone through the line, I had noticed grace and decided it was not for me. Grace was for losers, the soft, scared people who felt self-pity and needed to lean against someone bigger. God taught me, however, that grace is the starting point, the zero mile. It is where the Christian life begins, and I couldn't pass it by. I had to come to the place of admitting that all the good in me was a free, undeserved gift from God.

Even in relating this, I've faced the same tired monster of

self-sufficiency. I don't like to open up and bare myself to
the world. It hurts. I like to look good in front of people.
But God has taught me that He alone—not the crowd—is
the judge, and I can only become truly good if I submit to
Him and learn at His feet.

I shrink from becoming an answer man for Christians.
Who am I to give advice on raising children, marriage, or
any other problem? The safe way for me is to keep my
mouth shut, to avoid making my own marriage and family
vulnerable and scrutinized. But I'm free to take those risks
because of God's forgiving grace. In advance, He has accepted me with all my mistakes and limitations.

Grace frees me to go ahead with the ministry—not as a
means of impressing God, but as a way of expressing what
He has done for me. As 2 Corinthians 1:4 says: ". . . we
can pass on to them this same help and comfort God has
given us."

Learning to be a servant changed my outlook on my
ministry. The fat girls who came to me sobbing because of
their lack of self-control; the shy, stuttering guy who barely
mustered the strength to approach me; the protective, jealous parents who refused to hear their children's view-
points—these were not inferior people to be made perfect in my image. God was working in them. Once I accepted that, God brought me great joy and fulfillment in
sharing His life with them.

The ego trip was beginning to dissolve as I began to become a servant, not a master. I had expected this idea of
grace to make me feel lower, less worthy. But something
marvelous happened. Along with the realization of my hu-
manness came a flooding, cleansing experience of God's
forgiveness. I was loved! I didn't have to be constantly
rescuing the world. It's a lot like the billboard: YOU CAN
SLEEP. YOUR NATIONAL GUARD IS AWAKE. God is awake
and at work. Finally I could rest from trying to be God and
let Him love me. I was free to act, even to take rests and
make mistakes.

5

The Cripples Walk

*Christ has given me true dignity. You see, I am a son
of God . . . . I have the dignity that goes with being a
member of the royal family of God.*

TOM SKINNER

In her book *The Good Earth*, Pearl Buck told a beautiful story about a young couple in prerevolution China. It reminds me of the way I used to feel about God.

A Chinese boy named Wang Lung was reared in poverty. He never went to school. Almost from the time he could walk, he worked in the fields, trying to coax crops from the hard, cracked soil. Each day Wang Lung ate his bowl of rice, worked under the hot sun, and climbed wearily into bed at night.

Luck began to change for Wang Lung after he married young O-lan. He didn't choose her—Chinese peasants weren't allowed the luxury of falling in love. Instead, he bought her, sight unseen, out of slavery from one of the great houses of his village.

Wang Lung treated his new wife gruffly and without emotion as was the custom. He never complimented her, or conversed with her, or did things to please her. She was a worker, not a person to love.

Slowly, though, small splinters of feeling began edging into Wang Lung's marriage. His wife was slow, with square features and ugly unbound feet. Yet she rose every morning to fix tea for him and his father. She painstakingly rewove material to cover the holes in his clothes. She worked, un-complaining, all day long. Wang Lung softened, acting kinder.

Because of O-lan's thrift and her added hands in the field, Wang Lung soon began to save a little silver. He never spent it on fine things. He buried it under a clod of earth in his house.

The greatest joy came to Wang Lung's house with the birth of a son. O-lan had given the ultimate gift, and his house was blessed.

Wang Lung was bursting with pride as the New Year approached. He burned incense before the Buddhist gods and pasted red strips of good-luck paper on his farm tools. O-lan prepared special cakes like ones he had seen only on the tables of the great houses—colored cakes of rice flour, pork fat, and white sugar. The two were preparing for a visit back to the great house where O-lan had served as a slave.

On the second day of the new year, they dressed for the visit. O-lan wrapped the baby in a red coat and placed on him tiger-faced shoes and a red hat with a gilt Buddha sewn on front. She and Wang Lung wore new black coats of cotton.

Wang Lung could not hide his delight on this day. As he walked through the village with his boy child, his wife fol-lowing behind, men of the village would smile and speak to him with respect he'd never known before. How well he had done! In just a few years he had climbed to such a full life.

And then as he exulted, he was smitten with fear. What a foolish thing he was doing, walking like this under an open sky, with a beautiful man child for any evil spirit passing by chance through the air to see! He opened his coat hastily and thrust the child's head into his bosom and he said in a loud voice, "What a pity our child is a female whom no one could want and covered with smallpox as well! Let us pray it may die."

"Yes—yes," said his wife as quickly as she could, understanding dimly what a thing they had done.

As I look back over my walk as a Christian, I can see ways in which I dressed up my child to fool God. My situation was different than Wang Lung's. Wang Lung was trying to convince his gods his baby was flawed, out of fear. I was trying to *hide* flaws from God, because I didn't trust Him. I couldn't be honest with God. In our own ways we were both trying to fool God. We childishly assumed a few words and pretend masks would throw Him off the track.

When I'd come home exhausted and discouraged from a frustrating week of meetings, I couldn't let it show, even to God. Instead, I would grit my teeth, smile and say, "That was fun, Lord. What next?"

If I had a gnawing doubt about some quirk of doctrine I was supposed to believe, I wouldn't face it openly. I would shove it aside and try to fool God by pretending the doubt had never occurred. In addition, there were all sorts of issues beyond Scripture; yet I felt I couldn't question any part of the evangelical subculture. I was afraid to admit if I didn't agree with someone for fear I'd be drummed out of the corps. I could never admit, "I don't understand." I felt I had to have an answer for every question. I couldn't allow uncertainty or tenuousness.

In the late fifties and early sixties, for example, one flag of faith was ardent anti-Communism. Most of the evangelists had a stock speech, for certain crowds, about the Communist plan to take over the United States. We all quoted from one booklet called *The Communists' Master Plan,* describing how the United States, infiltrated and surrounded, would fall like a ripe plum into the hands of Communists in 1973. I had never seen the booklet, but accepted its existence and preached the sermons as an indispensable part of the Christian Gospel.

"I didn't see you and you didn't see me—O.K.?" (*Gahan Wilson*. Look *magazine*.)

I gave the anti-Communist speech near a university once, and for the first time in my career, I was called down hard. It took a strange, neglected university employee to shake me. He was considered the oddball of the campus though his only problem was a physical defect that affected his coordination so that he walked awkwardly and drooled slightly. He also claimed he was a card-carrying Communist. Most people avoided him.

After my speech, he came to me and said, "Jay, what were your sources for tonight's speech?" Cornered, I responded defensively, spinning out names and hearsay. He didn't argue, he just said, "Most of those sources don't exist."

Two days later he approached me with a list of 153 books with chapter and page references which exposed inaccuracies in my speech. He also handed me a bibliography of Reinhold Niebuhr. I had earlier presented a position paper on Niebuhr, calling him an untrustworthy neoorthodox. Afterwards he got me to admit I had never read Niebuhr. I'd only used secondary sources.

That embarrassing encounter taught me something about honesty. I had clung to statements from speeches by others without researching them. I couldn't summon the maturity needed to admit to the complexity of this issue. Like a child, I needed everything nailed down and labeled.

I began to see that I couldn't just float along mimicking other Christian speakers. I had to research and pray and struggle through Christian truth for myself. I had to gain intellectual honesty and integrity. I couldn't hide lazy shortcuts from God.

About that time a very significant book came out—*The Taste of New Wine* by Keith Miller. The message of this book hit me like a rush of fresh air. The author dared to expose himself as a frail, inconsistent human who had tasted God's grace, but needed much more feasting. Hundreds of similar books have followed Miller's style, but this first one made a powerful impact. Miller dared to suggest that we admit to God and to other Christians that we are nothing more than redeemed sinners. We are men, not competitors in a perfection contest.

My friends and I were like excited children learning to fly a kite. We had this marvelous, scary thing called honesty, and we were feeling out where we could go with it. In small clusters of two and three we started admitting our temptations and sins, exploring what it meant to "bear one another's burdens." Amazed, we discovered that we were commonly afflicted with the same doubts, depressions, and temptations to lust.

Those prayer meetings lasted far into the night. Since we all opened up, we no longer seized the opportunity to judge and reject one another. Rather, we determined to be true "fellowshippers." We felt washed clean. The cynicism and competition which had divided YFC melted into a group experience of loving concern.

Once we opened the door on the concept of honesty, we realized what a giant room we had been shut out of for so long. We always had seen honesty as a large, risky step that could anger God into retribution at any moment. Embarrassed, we realized that God could certainly handle it! He's known our thoughts all along. We had stymied ourselves by bottling up our inner beings, thus shutting off opportunities to deal with problems openly. We saw by contrast how lonely we had been, hiding ourselves from God.

As I read the Bible with new eagerness, I noticed the pattern of men of God. Jeremiah pleaded with God to give him a new assignment. David poured out his soul, confused and sometimes bitter, in psalms. Job questioned everything about God. Moses stammered and protested. These men all bared themselves before God, telling Him exactly how they felt. It seemed as though God delighted in feisty servants. He listened. He never rejected His children because of their unfitness. God can handle us. He stands above us, forgiving and beckoning us to higher things.

Perhaps the problem was in my view of sin. I acted as if I thought God's anger was directed against me for the punishment of my sin; so I vainly tried to hide my sins from Him. Actually, His anger is against the sin itself. He wants me freed from the sin, for my sake. He is not so much concerned with slapping me for what I did as with preventing me from being sucked into the same evil again.

God, of course, knows all truth at all times. At any moment He knows precisely how evil Jay Kesler is. By my fronts and hypocrisies I had only been deluding myself. The first wedges of honesty were merely a way of God teaching me what He already knew about me. When God asked Abraham to sacrifice Isaac, He was teaching Abraham about Abraham. God already knew the lesson.

The honesty germ proved contagious. It circulated and invaded other areas. I began to realize how dishonest I had been about self-image. I had split my self-concept into two parts. Deep down, I knew I must have some worth, because of the impact I was having on others and because God was using my gifts. But on the surface I could never admit to positive feelings about myself. To do so would be un-spiritual. Instead, I shyly responded to any compliment with an "Oh, that wasn't me speaking tonight, that was the Lord."

Paul Sartre blasted Christians for this trend in his play *The Flies*. In it, a man falls on his knees crying, "I stink! Oh, how I stink! I am a mass of rottenness . . . I have sinned a thousand times, I am a stink of ordure, and I reek to heaven." After this speech, Zeus, who stands for God, praises, "O worthy man!" Sartre is saying that this is how he sees Christians, groveling in the dust because of their sins. The more they do it, the more God is pleased. What a terrible caricature! This theology makes God big by making man small. But man is the zenith of God's Creation.

The Bible certainly preaches an awareness of the seri-ousness of sin. But just as strong as its emphasis on sin is the parallel emphasis on joyful, eternal forgiveness. God does not leave us groveling. At every turn He lifts us and cleanses our scabs and dresses us in new clothes.

As the truth of honesty and forgiveness permeated my life, I saw that many of the kids I was ministering to had terrible self-images. I traveled to Portland to speak at a rally, where a staff member had surveyed the audience be-fore I spoke. He found that the *average* kid in the audience had been to church six times a month! I had used these rallies as a platform for hellfire and brimstone sermons, without once considering my audience. I started looking at the kids in rallies. They were the same group of kids every time—the church kids. I also noticed that our preaching had crippled many of them.

We had beat on kids so long about sin and the need to be *separated* that they ended up truncated. They were the casualties of an evangelical overkill, programmed to go to every church meeting and every YFC rally and obey every petty Christian nuance. But they couldn't share their faith easily. Why? They had no friends. Their brand of Christianity had produced social misfits who could talk only to fellow Christians. Many of them weren't involved in sports or school activities—to do so would be worldly. The school kids labeled many of the Christians as losers, and the kids accepted the label. They thought it came with the martyrdom of being a Christian!

It amazes me to see that philosophy still surfacing today. It began with Greeks who split the world into fleshly (evil) and spiritual (good). But some people still define spirituality as "being more and more removed from the world." Religious communes sometimes take this idea to the extreme. In one California commune, only the leader can read something besides the Bible. He reads the newspaper each day to see what Bible prophecies are fulfilled. Beauty, sports, art, politics, and ecology are all worthless, according to this philosophy.

A historic meeting took place in YFC in which we faced this dilemma head-on, and what we discovered then brought about a revolution in the YFC approach. As we looked at the Bible, we saw the view of a separatist world disintegrating. Jesus was a very earthly Man. He contrasted Himself with John the Baptist, saying He was one who went to parties and ate and drank with the wrong people. When He prayed His last prayer for the disciples in John 17:15, He specifically said, "I do not ask you to take them out of the world" (TEV).

We came to a statement in Luke 2:52 which summarized everything the Bible tells us about Jesus' life between the time He turned twelve and His baptism by John the Baptist at age thirty. The verse is a brilliant, encompassing summary. "So Jesus grew both tall and wise, and was loved by God and Man."

First, we noticed, Jesus grew in wisdom—the sphere of

the mind. He grew in stature physically. He grew in favor with God and men—the spiritual and social dimensions. These four areas—mental, physical, spiritual, and social—were all important. It wasn't enough to grow in relationship to God. He made us so that we needed to grow physically, mentally, and socially also.

It sounds pretty basic. But the concept of the balanced life radically changed our thinking. It answered questions for kids, such as, "How can a Christian spend his time playing tennis?" and "Is it important to have non-Christian friends?" We structured our programs so that we could encourage growth in all four areas, not just the spiritual one.

The results were astounding. We saw kids smile, relax, open up. We attracted a broader spectrum of kids, as they began to see you didn't have to be weird to attend YFC meetings. We began to realize what the phrase "whole person" means.

I count this period as one of the greatest breakthroughs in Youth for Christ. For the first time, we didn't have to apologize for being human, for being alive. We could round out our aliveness through process with the freedom of the Gospel.

6

Discovering Me

One must have a place before one can give it up. One must receive before giving, exist before abandoning oneself in faith.

PAUL TOURNIER

There is something attractive about giving things up for God. As you can see throughout the pell-mell, frenetic first years of my ministry, I had emphasized "giving up." I gave up money, pride, family, fulfillment, happiness—everything I could think of, until I was empty. In this exhausted, hollow state I felt confused and bitter. I had given up everything for Christ. Why wasn't I more happy and fulfilled? The words of Paul Tournier cut right to the core. "Self-assertion must come before self-denial. We must first exist, defend ourselves, succeed, assert ourselves, before showing ourselves generous."

You have to have something before you give it.

I saw that I had never had myself. From conversion point on I had set my sights on the goals—clean living, witnessing, preaching—without going through the process of self-assertion that would give some content to my life. I hadn't yet accepted the idea of process, which holds that we don't become one-dimensional supermen when we become Christians.

One passage of Scripture impressed me with a wholly new view of humility—Philippians 2:5–8. "Your attitude

"I feel another attack coming on. Who am I? What am I doing
here?" (*By Charles E. Martin, reprinted from* The Saturday Evening Post, © *1950, The Curtis Publishing Company.*

should be the kind that was shown us by Jesus Christ, who,
though he was God, did not demand and cling to his rights
as God, but laid aside his mighty power and glory, taking
the disguise of a slave and becoming like men. And he
humbled himself even further, going so far as actually to die
a criminal's death on a cross."

As the prototype of humility, Jesus is seen stripping off
some of His prerogatives to come to earth. But note—His
change is not one of weakness to weakness. He leads from
strength, and deliberately takes on a position of weakness
by subjecting Himself to join humanity. Humility is not a
harsh "poor me" feeling of denial. It is a *choice,* a deliber-
ate decision to be a servant. Using Him as my model, I
realized that before I could minister, I needed to get control
of myself. To bring more Christians into the Kingdom, I
first needed to discover what *my* faith involved.

Was I preaching something I wasn't living? As I re-
flected, I found content lacking in my life. I needed to grasp

control of myself. Yes, God wanted me to sacrifice for Him, but He wanted a *living* sacrifice, one who had something of worth to sacrifice.

As I started with me, I found deficiencies. The balanced life my colleagues and I had so carefully devised was not my life. I realized, for instance, that we Christian leaders had constructed a false dichotomy between what was secular and sacred. Naturally, we participated in "secular" activities, such as fishing, driving a car, taking vacations, playing tennis, and gardening. But we always did so with our heads turned, looking back over our shoulders, wondering if God was displeased with our waste of time. After all, we could be out winning souls.

While at Taylor, I played basketball and volleyball with friends, but I never concentrated on the sport. Sports seemed unworthy and frivolous. I played to maintain friendships. "How can I enjoy playing ball against the background of a dying world?" I wondered. The fact is, I'm in better shape to help the dying world after learning to relax and recreate!

The Swiss psychiatrist Walter Trobisch said in *His* magazine that most Christians undergo two conversions. First, they are converted from the natural life and discover the supernatural; later, they rediscover the natural life from a redeemed viewpoint. Somewhere in the middle sixties, I experienced that second conversion.

This kind of split between the sacred and secular has afflicted ministers throughout history. John Wesley allowed no place for leisure, humor, and play. At his school, children rose for prayers at four in the morning, and couldn't play at all. George Whitefield, too, forbade enjoyment and once struck a child a number of blows when he struggled to remember the Lord's Prayer. But some men, such as D. L. Moody, found a balance. Moody raised hens for a hobby and specialized in practical jokes. He kept rubber fried eggs and fake potato chips in his cupboards to serve unsuspecting guests. Today, Billy Graham finds golf an important outlet from his busy schedule.

As I gingerly stepped into pursuits such as fishing and building a house without feeling guilty, I realized I, too, had been truncated. By being immersed in hustle and activity, I had shut out all opportunity for God's still, small voice. Sitting on the bank of a pond, watching a cork bob with the ripples, feeling the cool caress of moist air—I felt the relaxed sense of God's presence. In a lot of ways, my neighbors, unknowingly, had been better Christians than I. They had expressed interest in the neighborhood, visited the block, worked on rapport with their relatives. All this while I had flown around the country looking for larger crowds to reach. I hardly knew my wife and kids, much less my neighbors or more distant relatives.

I had been afraid to trust God with the world. On an airplane heading for yet another meeting, I read the little book by J. I. Packer, *Evangelism and the Sovereignty of God*. It sent shock waves through me. I realized how small my conception of God must be for me not to trust Him. I learned how much bigger than my realm of influence the world was, and I learned my simple, humble place in it. God was less interested in my potential than in me as a person. I had always thought He loved me for what I could do for Him, for my function. I had thought of myself as a pencil being shaped and shaved by some giant pencil sharpener in the Kingdom.

We are so used to judging people by their function. When I meet a stranger on an airplane, I immediately ask, "What do you do for a living?" If he says, "janitor," I interpret him one way. If he says, "I'm president of Bell Telephone," my entire view of him changes. In our society, I can't avoid pegging people by their functions and, sadly, valuing them because of their functions.

But God does not see His people like that. With God, people are never mere means, cogs in a machine, or functions. He sees us as His children. The TV series *Roots* showed Americans that even slaves who had been treated like sow pigs had inherent worth. They were not functions; they were people. That's why slaves created Negro spirituals such as "Nobody Knows the Trouble I've Seen." All around them society was saying, "You're worthless." But God loved them because of who they were: "Nobody knows like Jesus . . . ."

God loves me without strings attached. He made me with intrinsic worth. I saw a sign once: GOD DON'T MAKE NO JUNK. Accepting that brought me new life. Once I had a free self-concept, I wanted to turn it back to God, committing myself to Him.

Self-discovery also brought me in touch with my feelings. I had blotted out a large segment of the rainbow of emotions, thinking them inappropriate or even unspiritual. But the Jesus I read about in the New Testament *felt*. He showed joy at a wedding in Cana. He cried at Martha's grief. He agonized before God in Gethsemane, yearning for another way. He breathed fire at corruption in the temple. And what is most surprising—He never apologized for this range of emotions. He shared it with His disciples.

Some Christians seem to be specialists at denying emotions. We shy away from whatever might make us lose tight control of ourselves. (Compare the typical Protestant wedding to a Jewish, Slavic, or Arabian wedding.) We narrow our responses to a thin spectrum of nods and grimaces. The world, on the other hand, has a full range of emotions, but no meaning to attach to them. Non-Christian artists feel the despondency and despair of the human condition, and express them brilliantly, but without interpretation. They also feel the joy and ebullience of life, but can't find the rationale for it. Existential plays shout this confusion. The poets beautifully capture the crashing emotions of modern life, but leave them untagged, unattached.

I began to see the role of Christians as analogous to that

of Helen Keller's teacher, Annie Sullivan. She, too, found a student with a whole range of sensations. Helen could feel the vibrations of a train going by, the hot pavement against her bare feet, the pelting wetness of rain. But she had no grid through which to interpret these sensations; so they had no meaning. She was buffeted by the world, yet cut off from understanding it.

Modern man feels the world deeply—the agony and the ecstasy of being alive. But he needs a teacher to explain. Helen's teacher, Annie, painfully began the process of teaching Helen how to spell. By forming letters of the alphabet with her fingers placed against Helen's palms, Annie taught her to imitate a sequence and thus spell out words. To Helen it was just another game. Annie could never get it across that the game had relevance to her experience in the world. A bridge was missing, until one bright, warm day in April, 1887.

"This morning, while she was washing," Annie wrote, "she wanted to know the name for water. We went out to the pumphouse, and I made Helen hold her mug under the spout while I pumped. As the cold water gushed forth, filling the mug, I spelled w-a-t-e-r in Helen's free hand. The word coming so close upon the sensation of cold water rushing over her hand seemed to startle her."

Amazed, Helen dropped her mug and held out her hand as Annie spelled the word again. Helen smiled, then reached down and pounded her fist on the ground, holding out her hand for Annie to spell a new word. Then came the pump, then a trellis. At last Helen pointed to Annie herself and learned t-e-a-c-h-e-r. She gleefully repeated the word in Annie's hand.

Somehow Annie had spanned that bridge between sensation and meaning.

The world, beleaguered by unclaimed sensations, begs for a framework of truth to interpret both the yearning for utopia and the slide toward evil. We have the answers in the Gospel. But unless we learn to feel with the world, experiencing the human condition in its fullness, we cannot be teachers.

God taught me to cry at death, to laugh deeper, to live with anticipation and awe. Only by learning that could I truly reach out to my neighbors.

Perhaps the most important aspect of self-discovery I am learning has to do with members of the Body of Christ ministering to one another. *Psychology Today* has run reports on experiments which show how self-image changes in different groups. For example, one group of control persons is asked a series of questions about themselves by a suave, obviously successful person. Another group is asked the same questions by a rather bored, ineffectual questioner who conveys an air of inferiority. Invariably the latter group rates themselves higher, because their self-image is raised by the contrast to the questioner.

In other experiments, teachers are told that certain members of a class are superior in intelligence, while in fact they are normal. Because of the different way these students are treated due to the teacher's expectations, they perform better.

We have great power in affecting those around us. That power is heightened in the Body of Christ because of the spiritual warfare we're in. For me to grow honestly, I need other members of the Body with whom I can share and open up, trusting them to affirm me. For my own development, I need to reach out and give to other people.

One of the great joys of my life has come in the last few years since our family has joined a church in Geneva, Illinois. There, I am not Jay Kesler, president of Youth for Christ. I am Jay Kesler, a believer with certain gifts and certain needs. I can learn from those caring persons around me. For example, I have a surgeon friend who devotes as much care and attention to playing basketball with his son as he does to sewing up a patient. I learn from the process of growing close to him.

The Bible says, ". . . perfect love casts out fear . . ." (1 John 4:18 RSV). Friendship bears that out. As I expose risk to a friend and he still accepts and affirms me, I grow stronger.

Psychologist Thomas Malone of the Atlanta Psychiatric Clinic says he meets two kinds of people. One group is unhealthy and studded with inadequacies. The members of the group walk around crying, "Please love me; please love me." The other group are the persons whole enough to be lovers. He says that the best cure for the first group is to heal them to the point where *they* can be lovers and helpers of others. If they reach the place of being helpers, they will automatically fill the deep needs for attention and love inside them.

It's a paradox, this mix of having and giving, and learning to have love through learning to give it. That's why I think love will always be a process. We'll always be wearing a STILL UNDER CONSTRUCTION sign as we move among fellow believers.

7

Coming Home

In the last ten years I have come to understand how, through the Gospels, we can see God in the shape of a man, and a man in the shape of God, thereby grasping what I think is the most wonderful concept of all—of God as a father . . . .

MALCOLM MUGGERIDGE

I had been preaching a good many years when a meeting was canceled, giving me unexpected free time with my family. I cruised home that evening, singing to myself in the car, imagining how thrilled Janie and the three little ones would be. What would be a normal evening to many men—shoes off, reading the newspaper, playing with the kids—was a rare delicacy to me.

As I pulled into the driveway, I half expected my young family to stream out the front door, squealing with delight, and clamor around me. No one came. *Oh, well,* I thought, *they could be in the backyard, or maybe the vacuum's running, and they didn't hear me.* When I opened the door, I did get a hug and surprised greetings, but Janie quickly excused herself to the bedroom. Confused and hurt, I followed her. She was changing clothes, preparing to go shopping.

"Honey, do you have to go tonight?" I asked. "I was looking forward so much to a relaxing evening with you and the kids."

She glanced up, surprised at the tone of my voice and said, "Why not? I had planned to go out. Why should I change my plans?"

I protested feebly for a few minutes, and then she said something that knifed deeply. "After all, Jay, we don't really need each other."

Janie left on her shopping trip, and I did a slow burn all evening. I felt rejected, unloved, and misunderstood. The kids went to bed, and I plunked down in an armchair, staring glumly at the flickering TV all evening. Deep down, I knew Janie was right. She had given me a perfect one-sentence description of our relationship.

Every year since our wedding I had spent at least 200 nights away from home. I had the hotel receipts to prove it. I had missed the joy of my children's births—all three had come while I was away. How could we need each other? We weren't together that much.

I was too wounded to talk it out with Janie that night, but what she had said gnawed at me during the next few months of traveling and speaking. I began to see how our marriage looked through her eyes—about twenty-eighth on my prior-

ity list. And I couldn't get away from the clear commands in
Scripture that a minister should first see that his own house
is in order.

Not long after that I received a call from a close friend in
Texas. He was an enthusiastic youth worker who had married a beautiful and energetic college grad. I had participated in their wedding ceremony. His voice had a tone of
sudden urgency. "Jay, you've got to come," he said. "My
wife just left me. She said she won't talk to anyone but
you."

I dropped a few meetings from my schedule and flew
down to try to patch the rift. Prepared with my list of scrip-
tural injunctions, I visited his wife. I ran into a stone wall.
"Don't give me Bible verses," she said. "It took me seven
years to work up the courage to leave him. He's bludgeoned
me with those verses like 'Wives, submit,' since our wedding day. He's married to his work and to his own ego, not
to me. I'm just a prop to make his life easier. If God is his
God and Christ is his Christ, then . . . then I want to go to
hell!"

We talked for hours. I tried to pray with her; I tried to
bring the two together. But she wouldn't budge, and I left
for home defeated and disturbed. A bright, seemingly ideal
marriage had soured. Both my friend and his wife would
bear permanent scars.

On the flight back to Chicago, I felt tired and depressed. I
had brought a book to read on the flight, but my mind was
spinning with the trauma and emotional attacks I had just
heard. I looked down at the thousands of tiny houses. Some
were surrounded by patches of green and squares of neatly
planted crops. Some were clustered in small towns with a
church, a school, and a store. Those in cities were jammed
together in rows with barely a crack in between. I thought
of all the family units down there. Some were humming like
a well-oiled machine. Others were creaking along in a state
of disrepair. Some families had already shattered apart and

"Well, today I dreamed the impossible dream, and it was impossible, all right." (*Drawing by Stevenson;* © *1977, The New Yorker Magazine, Inc.*)

had joined again with parts of other shattered units.

I thought, too, of the Christian families I knew. Many of the severely split homes of which I was aware belonged to Christian leaders.

Why? Why do men who study Scripture and spend hours praying and preaching God's love fall apart in their own homes? "We don't need each other," Janie had said. I had always used the excuse, "But, Honey, I'm serving Jesus." Could time spent with her also be serving Jesus? Had I ever conveyed that to her?

Before his immersion into the drug culture, Timothy Leary did extensive studies on the types of personalities attracted to the pastorate. He called the general type of person the "top dog." For example, a narcissist "top dog" may unconsciously use his ministry to feed his own unmet needs. He impresses others with his suaveness and attractiveness in the pulpit, fishing for approval and compliments. He ranks spiritually.

Threatened by the admiring attention he gets, his wife may react in several ways. She may compete with his admirers. Or, resentful, she may demean him and communicate a just-who-do-you-think-you-are? feeling. Or, she may withdraw and become less dependent on him.

I had to ask myself, was I using my ministry as a device to fill my own feelings of inadequacy? With practice, it became easy to turn on an excitable crowd of teenagers who thought I was a Christian celebrity. Was I relying on them to fill needs I should be allowing my family to meet?

I decided my family was worth *any* investment. I needed to learn to need Janie and my children and let them know I needed them.

I no longer tell my wife and kids I'm serving Jesus when I leave for the airport. I tell them I'm going to work, just like the IBM salesman down the street. If they blame anyone for my absence, I want them to blame the company, not Jesus. And I've also learned that serving Jesus might take the form of pushing a grocery cart on Saturday morning or washing dishes at night.

I've begun to look upon my family as a proving ground for everything I believe. If I can't make it work within my family, I might as well stop preaching it.

Above anything else, I want my family to glow with acceptance. I've discussed self-image and the need to develop a self-concept. As I've watched healthy families and sick families, I've seen that the family is the perfect place to develop—or to destroy—a person's self-image. The family is a visible incarnation of God's grace.

I believe God created the family as a central carrier of the godly value system. Consider the other institutions in this world: government, corporations, schools, armies. All are based on status and competition. You rise in them by proving your greater worth. Your business succeeds when you prove your product is better and you outsell the competition. In the army, your worth is determined by the stripes on your sleeve. Guys with few stripes take orders. Guys with many stripes give orders and live in plusher quarters. The entire world system is built on competition, on the struggle of the fittest.

Against this background, God carves out a unit called the family, which you join just by being born. A retarded son has as much worth as a genius. His acceptance in the family is not questioned. He deserves love simply because he was born and bears the family name. The prodigal son who squanders his father's riches is welcomed as eagerly as his older brother who followed all the rules.

When I ask people what they do in life, I sometimes get "justa" responses: "I'm justa housewife"; "I'm justa janitor"; or "I'm justa shy person." There should be no justas in a family. A family is not an earned status. It's not a status at all; it's a birthright.

Love and acceptance must characterize the Christian family. But as I've talked to kids who are having trouble with their parents, often they indicate the family is the place where they feel least accepted. Their peers, fellow Christians, and teachers accept them. But their parents don't because of their clothes, school grades, their tastes in music.

Those differences aren't imagined; they're real. So how can a Christian family cope with them? My kids have taught me that the tensions parents and their children go through are potentially explosive. I've been to many stress camps in YFC, but I can't think of a tougher stress camp than the one at home. Getting kids up, fed, teeth brushed, on the way to school—and doing it every day—that's a job! And it lasts twenty years or so, unlike the strain of a week of backpacking. All the while, I'm under economic stress, job tension, and social pressure. All us Keslers are guarding our rights—our territorial imperatives—and clanking our varied temperaments together.

Under these pressures, what should be the goal of a family? Should it strive to remove the stresses? It can't be done, unless you run your family as a military platoon, with your barking orders and their marching in formation. How many teenagers would endure that?

The beauty of a family is in allowing all the members to work out these glaring stresses under the protective umbrella of acceptance and prayer. American culture, with its independent nuclear families, complicates that process. Unlike extended families, we cut off the wisdom of grandparents, create emotional distance between cousins, and carve out a tiny, close-knit society of four or six or more. That heightens stress.

God fits into this growth process by giving us a set of guidelines to work from and by providing a source for the love needed in the give-and-take clashes. Teenagers will invariably rebel and parents will invariably overreact. But a Christian family has a unity of belief that can survive such bumps.

After thinking through the concepts of grace and how it helps me live through life in process, I came across some remarkable research by Merton Strommen's Youth Research Center in Minneapolis. Strommen seems to have validated through meticulous research that the battleground of legalism versus grace may be the most crucial factor in a Christian home.

In an intriguing study, Strommen randomly selected a thousand high-school youths nationwide from an evangelical denomination. While each of these youths was answering 200 survey questions on concerns about his family, his parents in another room responded to the same questions *as they thought their child was answering them.*

Strommen figured that if a parent and child answered similarly, it would indicate a degree of closeness and understanding between parent and teenager. A parent in close touch with his child's feelings and attitudes is, after all, better able to cope with them.

If, however, the parent's and youth's answers were widely divergent, they could be strangers to each other.

Strommen used a correlation scale of 0 to 1 to reflect the range of similarity. If a parent predicted every one of his teenager's responses, he would have scored 1. In fact, one parent correlated so perfectly he received a .99. Some parents misunderstood their children so severely that they received negative scores, indicating they predicted the *opposite* of their child's actual response.

At the end of each survey, the researchers asked the participants to complete a sentence. For the parent: "My relationship with my teenager is _____." For the teenager: "My relationship with my parent is _____."

As you might expect, the parents who had predicted a high percentage of their teenagers' responses had the best relationships with their teenagers. An understanding parent who accurately perceives his child can better meet his needs and relate more cordially.

Some responses were shocking. One teenager, the child of a poorly correlating parent, wrote: "My mother is a witch, a snob, and a nosy Holy Roller. I despise her." The mother showed incredible lack of perception by saying, "My relationship with my teenager is a good one. We are close, and I feel she often confides in me and desires to please. We are pals." (Undoubtedly, if the daughter exploded in anger and left home, the mother would be confused and hurt. She had completely misread her teenager.)

One of Strommen's most fascinating findings surfaced when he explored what effect the parents' religious faith had on the relationship with their teenager. (Remember, all teenagers were evangelical churchgoers.) Strommen studied the 150 parent-teenager groupings which showed the lowest correlation factor and compared them to the 150 with the highest correlation. He concludes: "The two groups were very much alike in most areas under comparison (e.g., socio-economic level, educational background, religious involvement, etc.). Where they differed markedly was in their perception of the Christian faith. Low-correlating parents tended to view Christianity as a religion of works—something one did. The high-correlating parents tended to view Christianity as a religion of grace—something one accepts as a gift."

Strommen continued: "A committed, intrinsic Christian faith is best communicated by adults who are not only accurate in their empathetic relationships *but also Gospel oriented in their faith.* In other words, openness and perceptiveness with respect to one's children are highly associated with a similar religious faith in young people."

If I understand Strommen's research correctly, he has come up with a devastating question for us as evangelical parents. Have we, in our insistence on rules and regimentation, missed the whole concept behind the family? It is a serious question, for our idea of a family must be firmly rooted in Scripture, and Scripture plainly denounces the type of law-oriented faith which Strommen uncovered. Could it be that teenagers are rejecting their parents' faith because it is a faith based on works and not on grace?

Because of this concept of grace and forgiveness, a Christian family can also be conscious of the growth process. It has goals to work toward. If a family member bursts into tears, or a TV show affects a child, or someone loses his temper, these crises present learning situations. It doesn't help to steel yourself and pretend nothing happened. Crises allow growth and maturity.

One of my natural tendencies as a parent is to patch up each problem. It's easier to pick up my son's socks than to go through the hassle of teaching him. Likewise, it's easier to fix up the family car after an accident than to teach responsibility and ask him to work for the required money.

When a daughter becomes pregnant, I've seen parents

"buy off" the crisis with a quick abortion, refusing to discuss the matter with the girl and face up to the crisis. God does not teach us by fixing up things for us. He allows us to learn from our mistakes as free people. I believe the family should reflect that same stance toward crises—they are opportunities to learn truth.

If a family can learn love, acceptance, and growth, a strange thing happens. Doors open for the family to become the world's best educational tool. In my case, I had to re-earn my family's trust. I had to prove that I needed them and they were important enough for me to make them a high priority. Once I did that and had earned their trust, the opportunities were enormous.

Lloyd Ogilvie tells a moving story which symbolizes what a family can be. When he was growing up, a little boy in the neighborhood suffered brain damage in an automobile accident. Doctors said the only hope for him to walk, run, and play again would be a repatterning of the brain.

For several hours each week the children of the neighborhood would take turns working with the little boy's arms and legs. As they did so, new grooves were being formed in the brain that would eventually enable him to use his limbs again. Ogilvie describes the excitement each child felt when the boy regained his ability to walk. Each had been, in a loving way, a part in teaching how to grow. The family is the best place where in a cocoon of warmth and love, we can be taught and repatterned in the ways of God. I've talked to a number of kids and adults who are living in communes, and it has struck me that what some of these people are seeking is the environment they missed by not being in God's kind of family. I want my family to be so accepting and loving, that its members can learn from each other without being threatened.

The kind of acceptance I've learned has no place for acts of distrust such as looking in children's drawers and opening their mail. And I've learned not to say things such as,

"If you were a good Christian, you wouldn't do that!" Good Christians *do* hit their sisters and disobey. What's at stake is not the child's worth as a person or as a Christian—it's his specific behavior at that moment, and that's the issue with which I should deal.

If a family succeeds at becoming that unit of acceptance in the midst of a harsh world, it offers a base for its members to learn how to grow through pain and process.

As I look back on my own childhood, I can see the importance of learning to cope with pain. My father went through a lot of struggle. In the depression my father packed everything he owned in his Model T and moved to Wisconsin to get a land grant. He first set up his family in a hay storage barn, and then improved to a tent. He worked in a sawmill, trading his labor for lumber to build a log cabin. After swapping his Model T for two mules, he hand cleared forty acres and tried becoming the first farmer that far north to keep hogs and chickens through the winter.

I was born in that setting—on a hand-built table in the middle of the log cabin. Some winters my Dad worked all day to chop enough firewood to keep the cabin warm. For the first years Dad fought a losing battle against a harsh environment.

Later, he chose to be a union leader, a most unpopular position at that time. One night he was called to return to the factory. When he arrived he found no one—just a dark parking lot surrounded by a chain-link fence. He waited nervously for a moment, then, suspicious, called some union friends. Within minutes he heard footsteps and the clang of a gate shutting. Four men had surrounded him, threatening him with clubs and chains, before his union friends arrived and rescued him. He ran into scenes like that often: water hoses, the wrath of management, strike-breaking violence.

Because of these experiences, I did not grow up thinking

life would be comfortable or pain free. In fact, I grew up with a perception of life weighed more on the side of its cruelty. But it seldom got my father, or us kids, down. I think I know the reason now. Our family was a haven. It was filled with love and acceptance. As my father struggled with crops that would never grow on rocky, hard soil or came home after discouraging battles with labor and management, he always found a place to lick his wounds and gain strength for the next battle. We were his kingdom, his castle of strength.

As we children went out to meet our own struggles with competition and status, we knew each night when we came home that we would be accepted and loved and refreshed. In our hearts, we knew pain and suffering couldn't beat us. We had each other. It may sound like "The Waltons," but it was true. The media has somehow made such family solidarity seem an impossible ideal.

Like every child, I went through periods of rebellion when I rejected my family. But I realize what a wonderful legacy my father and mother left me. And I realize the true function of a family. It gives an environment to allow us to cope with the process of life.

Now that I am a father, I can see the marvelous wisdom in God's design for a family. As I leaf through Scripture, I am amazed at the number of times God uses the family as an analogy for expressing His truth. Deep in the construction of society, I think He has inextricably wound together the threads of human family and spiritual growth. The closer my family comes to the model He set up, the easier it will be for my children to embrace Christian truth. The closer I come to being the ideal father, the easier it will be for my children to accept the Father.

I believe families teach us something about the nature of the universe. I don't think God chose the term *Father* arbitrarily. He could have chosen many other terms, and the

Bible does list other models, such as God the King. Yet time and again, God seems to rely on the word *Father* to convey His truth. Almost half of the human population become fathers, and the word carries meaning in every culture.

It helps me, in my approach to God, to think through the analogy of Fatherhood. Sometimes I reflect on what my children could best do to please me. I'll think back over the things they've done. I have a dresser drawer full of treasures—poems, cards, essays my kids have made for me. Each one of these has a very special meaning, and it gives me great thrills to sift through them.

It also pleases me when my kids obey me. My kids can learn from me about the purpose of rules in the same way that I learn about the purpose of God's rules. We once lived on a busy street, and I had a rule that our kids could not ride their bikes in the street. That was okay for a while, but gradually I heard, "But, Dad, the other kids in the neighborhood all get to ride their bikes in the street!"

Tension resulted, and I sometimes overheard my kids talk about how unreasonable their parents were on this issue. Then one day a child was struck by a car on our street. All at once my kids understood that maybe there was something to our rules—maybe our rules were constructed out of love for them, and love does not always mean constant happiness.

When I think about the ways my children have pleased me, I always come to the same conclusion. What would please me most as a father is for my children to love each other and to grow up with rightness and truth instilled in them. I don't want them to obey me just because they know the consequences. I want it to become a part of their lives. By learning that, it's easier for me to trust God when He sets down some principles I may not understand. It's easier for me to see why I need a God I can turn to as a child. By experiencing my family, I come more in touch with the truth of the universe.

In the church there is a lot of talk these days about the Body of Christ. I read books and hear sermons on the parts of Christ's body and other metaphors used in Scripture. The one that rings true for me, though, is the family. I believe that if you had no other revelation than a model family and a hint that it was an analogy of truth, you could come up with a fair picture of God and the way He wants us to relate.

This chapter began with a statement by Malcolm Muggeridge. In his book *Jesus Rediscovered,* Muggeridge expands on that statement:

> Only in the last ten years I have come to understand how, through the Gospels, we can see God in the shape of a man, and a man in the shape of God, thereby grasping what I think is the most wonderful concept of all—of God as a father and of the human race as a family: not equal, as political idealists like to pretend, not at all, but equal as brothers and sisters in a family are equal. Some are clever, some are stupid, some are attractive, some are boring, some are ugly, some are beautiful; all this is true, but the moment that you have a sense of family and a father these differences become insignificant, as they do in a family, and all are equal. No one in a family would say that a plain sister is inferior to a pretty one; not inside a family, only outside.

I am convinced that God primarily commissions His servants with an awesome responsibility—to produce a working model of His love and unity as a Kingdom to stand against the hatred and struggle of life.

Christian families spread across a society can be the salt of the earth, little settlements of God's value system in a world falling apart. They are like an archipelago, linked together by a commitment to another Kingdom and each providing a miniculture for those values to be passed on through generations.

As such, the family demands all the energy and attention I can give it. It is, after all, my creation. When I dare to become a father, it constitutes the closest I ever come to living out the image of God.

8

Two Worlds

I and my God lived in one world, a specially arranged world, where everything made sense. All around me were the agonies of real life. But I didn't see them. I turned my gaze toward God.

INGMAR BERGMAN
Winter Light

Four of us were gathered around a wooden crib. Two young parents were sniffling and yet smiling through their tears. My wife Janie and I were squeezing each other's hand tightly. A newly Christian couple with simple faith had asked us over for prayer.

This was no ordinary prayer. We were surrounding a four-year-old boy who was sleeping peacefully, unaware of the intense emotion crackling in his room. The boy had leukemia, and doctors had given him only a few more months to live. Soon his chubby little body would swell, and he would spend night after night screaming with pain.

I barely knew this couple, but they had heard I was speaking in the area and had contacted me. They looked at me with such hope and trust. They had read accounts of healings in the Bible and were convinced their son could live.

Fighting back the lump in my throat, I prayed aloud, affirming to God we believed He could use this child on earth and could preserve Him if He wanted. The prayer was not profound—just a simple request to the Father.

But underneath I was praying a desperate plea to God. It went like this: "Lord, you see this dear young couple with such fragile new faith. They could easily reject all they believe if this verbal prayer falls empty. Please, Lord, help me out. What do I say to them? Please make this one a genuine healing!"

Janie and I left, drained after that traumatic prayer meeting. Six months passed before we heard again from the young couple. They sent a letter which said doctors believed their son was healed. They could find no trace of leukemia.

Thirteen years later I got another letter. It began: "You may not remember the incident, but you shared our sorrow one day in Iowa. Now we want you to share our joy. Our son just graduated from high school. His health is beautiful."

I have seen miracles. Some illnesses have been evidently healed. I have seen people changed from alcoholics and drug addicts into genuine, loving Christians.

But I have also seen my own brother-in-law writhing bravely on his deathbed with cancer, gasping to squeeze out one more breath. And I've seen rebellious kids who do not respond to their parents' love and marriages which collapse despite prayer and counseling.

How do I put these experiences together? Why do I sometimes doubt God? How can I trust Him? I once tried to hide doubt, to suppress it beyond view, because I thought it must be sin. As I've let my fears show, though, I've discovered that almost every Christian I've talked to experiences the same piercing questions. My doubt comes in waves at weak moments, then it may depart and leave me alone for months. How do these doubts fit into the process of Christian growth? Can I ever escape them?

We are supernaturalists in a naturalist world and culture. Yes, it's changing with the influx of witches, Ouija boards, and books on exorcism, but they're still considered freakish, abnormal. To my world of desks, telephones, and typewriters, the supernatural seems distant.

From theologians, from writers, from filmmakers, we have all heard about the silence of God. It has prompted some to say He is dead. Most of us Christians have seen brief, unquestionable glimpses of His presence. But still the doubt returns. I serve a faceless God. No one alive has ever seen Him. Most of the time He works in ways that could be open to more than one interpretation. He never lights His name in the sky for me to see.

So I live, believing, but sometimes doubting. I once read a sermon on the fourth commandment, "Thou shalt not take the name of the Lord thy God in vain." The author suggested that verse means much more than swearing. To him, it means living as though God doesn't exist. The taking of God's name means I have to somehow live in an awareness of His presence and His power. He must be a steady, conscious part of my daily life. As a Christian, I have taken on the name of God. Why, then, do my prayers sometimes seem vacant, foolish? Why do I inwardly yearn for more outward, sure signs of His presence?

I seldom have these doubts in a group of Christian friends. They come, instead, when I'm alone—often when I'm tired and vulnerable. At their most severe, they make me wonder whether I'm just playing games in my faith. Are my acts of preaching, praying, and witnessing mere charades?

If you never have those fleeting thoughts, please skip this chapter. But I suspect that at some time, most Christians do. We tend to rely on learned patterns and on peer pressure for our Christian behavior. We can keep on acting "Christian" without even thinking, and the voice of God can fade into the background.

My problem is that I want God to act *my* way. I want the world to be black and white, with all Christians exhibiting an undeniable supernaturalism. I want to be able to point to every occurrence and say, "That's God" or "That's the devil." But life is not like that. It's confusing and mixed up. My purest moments are tainted with selfishness and sin.

God has chosen to act in a veiled way in history. The Bible records pulses of His direct activity—large clumps of miracles such as those in the exodus and those surrounding the Incarnation. But in a day like ours we are left with glimmers and hints. We see through a glass darkly. To shed light on this problem, it has helped me to go through Scripture and get a clearer picture of the way God works in the world. Doing so has strengthened my belief and given me a rationale to fall back on in times of doubt.

One of the clearest facts I find in the Bible is that history is being lived on two levels. In a few spots in the Bible the veil is lifted, and we can see how the two levels are affecting each other. An intriguing example of this is recorded in Daniel 10. Daniel began a fast and prayed for some clear guidance and explanations from God. He continued fasting for three weeks, awaiting an answer. Finally, an angel came in a vision. The angel quickly explained that God had sent him on the first day of Daniel's fast, but it took him three weeks and the assistance of Michael to break through the defenses of a spirit prince! Here two seemingly separate levels of history are brought together, and the actions of one have direct bearing on the other. Daniel prayed for help and got no immediate response, but later found supernatural help had been on the way all the time.

In 2 Kings 6 another strange incident is recorded. The Syrian armies had been stymied in their pursuit of Elisha and the king of Israel. Then, they caught up. Elisha awoke one morning to face a great army of chariots and horses.

With incredible confidence he said to his servant, "Don't be afraid, for our army is bigger than theirs!" Then the Lord opened his servant's eyes to the horses of fire and chariots of fire everywhere on the mountain. Somehow the grim world of spears and stabbings and marches and chariot charges was also attended by an equally real world of spirit warfare. Events on the human level of history did not take place apart from this higher level, at least in these unusual instances. The two levels worked together.

Jesus' comment that angels rejoice at one sinner's repentance likewise pulls together the levels of history. Acts on earth which may seem normal, even dull, have cosmic significance. Our Christian acts of prayer, loving each other, sharing faith with others, worshiping, and relieving suffering just don't seem different enough to convince someone that Christianity is true. Yet, because of this hidden level of history, they *matter*.

It's one thing to believe in the existence of these two levels of history (most Christians acknowledge the fact). It's quite another to try to put them together. Usually on earth we think we are dealing only with the lower level. I live out my life immersed in the visible world. Supernatural conversion comes through natural channels such as a sermon on the radio or the witness of a neighbor.

But by its nature, my faith rests in an unseen world. That complicates arguments when I talk to a skeptic. Anthropologists say that if you take a black-and-white photo to a primitive tribe in South America or West Irian and show it to a tribesman, he can't interpret it. He can see wavy lines, and shadows, and shades of gray. But he can't make the quantum leap that allows him to see the much larger world those lines and shadows represent. He has no experience in projecting a three-dimensional world from those two-dimensional scratchings.

His inability to see, of course, does nothing to affect the

"Okay, if there's no God, who changes the water?" (*G. H. Rosen—from* The Princeton Tiger.)

existence of that real world. Those of us who understand photography, images, and symbols can translate it. But we can only do so because we've been equipped.

To a skeptic (and to me in moments of doubt), my words and inflections and pleas in prayer may seem shallow, empty actions with no significance. But behind those acts lies a deeper level of reality. C. S. Lewis dealt with this phenomenon beautifully in his outstanding essay "Transposition." He used several examples to illustrate how "natural" faculties can contain and express the supernatural. For example, he says when you try to analyze the physical sensations behind emotions—what your *body* actually feels—a kick or flutter in the diaphragm may express both joy and anguish. Physically, you may have the same sensation when you win a great award or when you are terribly frightened. Your face flushes; your pulse races; your stomach churns. But those physical sensations represent something entirely different, on a much richer level of emotion.

In the same way, those events we experience which look

natural and common can be partaking in something that is supernatural. Though my emotions at conversion were strong, physically they were not so different from other emotions I had experienced. That fact does not diminish their reality as a channel for supernatural experience.

In fact, as I look back over God's working, it seems that He almost prefers to work through means which to the observer seem least supernatural. For example, consider the Incarnation of Christ, the most startling event of history. Yes, some miracles did occur: the Virgin Birth, some dreams, a bright star, frightened shepherds. But on the whole, the first Christmas was a fairly normal day, as seen from the natural perspective. A girl was pregnant for nine months. There was a tiresome journey for a census, a humble birth in a stable, a few animals. A few shepherds came, but there was little fanfare. The Son of God came quietly. *What's so big?* a scoffer may ask.

Behind the scenes, however, God had been working for centuries. Alexander the Great had conquered much of the world and taught it Greek. The Romans wrested control from Greece and built a superb system of roads and commerce which Paul would use. A government census forced a difficult journey, so Jesus could be born in Bethlehem. Thousands of factors which had no obvious supernatural significance came together at the precise point in history when Christianity was born.

God's Son could have come as a blazing, alien creature in a space suit. Instead, God chose to send Him through nine months of fetal development and thirty-three years of human growth, in a body just like the ones wrapped around us. God could have sent the Bible on chrome tablets in a kryptonite trunk. Instead, he fleshed it out through stubborn humans over hundreds of painstaking years.

To be honest, I also have to admit that a spectacular display of God's power won't necessarily convince the world. Take the ten plagues of Egypt, for example. Cecil B. DeMille spent millions to imitate them, and his film sequences still look phony. Even the real events failed to convince the pharaoh at first. Or how about the Resurrection of Jesus? More than five hundred people attested that He had come back from the dead, but many refused to believe them. God Himself walked on earth for thirty-three years, teaching and performing astounding miracles. Yet, of those who heard Him, only a minority believed.

As I've contemplated these things, I've concluded that what makes me yearn for miraculous proof is my lack of faith. I want God to conduct well-orchestrated, televised miracles, so I can invite all my friends over to see an act of God they can't deny. I want to escape from living *in process* and live in a world where I've already arrived. After all, if God *proves* Himself to me in a spectacular way . . . that's not faith. Faith means believing in the unseen, the hoped for. The methods God chooses are just as real, just as supernatural, but they always require that slippery element of faith. God leaves me in an unresolved tension which demands maturity. The dilemma pushes me to one of His two options—to reject or accept Him.

To non-Christian observers, I must seem awfully foolish. I restrain my passions; I suffer; I go through strange rituals of worship and obedience—all the time stoutly declaring that there really is an unseen world out there. It's a risk. I do, however, get one unquestionable advantage over the scoffer. I have hope—real hope.

I can believe that one day every bruise, every leukemia cell, every embarrassment and hurt will be set right, and all those grim moments of hoping when all seemed hopeless will be rewarded. God is not finished yet. When He finally does let out the stops, and pulls together the two levels of history in a way that nobody can deny, all will be set straight.

I have no proof, but I have hope. God never quite does believe for me. He respects me too much; that step is mine.

William Golding's novel *Lord of the Flies* symbolizes what will happen someday. The story begins when a passenger plane crashes on a jungle island, leaving only English schoolboys as survivors. They naturally choose a leader and go about the business of building shelters and seeing to a fire. One boy, Jack, sneaks off from the group, looking for more exciting thrills. Gradually, one by one, a whole cluster of boys slips away and joins Jack. Instead of the orderly world of signaling and waiting for rescue, they plunge into exotic, evil rituals of pig hunts and chants. Soon they use the pigs' heads speared on the ends of sharp sticks as idols to worship. Losing all inhibitions, the boys paint their faces and snake in wild dances. They completely ignore the larger world they came from, and immerse themselves in this exotic new one.

Ralph, the former leader, tries to continue with the small band of boys who remained with him. But it gets harder. One of his boys is "accidentally" murdered by one of Jack's warriors. Soon all order breaks down, and Ralph is pursued by the screaming painted band of savages. They chase him with spears and clubs, waving one stick, sharpened on both ends, reserved for Ralph's head. Ralph frantically runs the length of the island, hunting for an escape. At last, exhausted, he falls, waiting for the pain of a grisly death.

Instead, when he looks up, he sees a foot, a creased pair of pants, and a jacket covered with brass buttons. He looks full into the face of a uniformed officer of the British navy. The fierce warriors collapse in shame. Once again they are spoiled boys playing evil games. Their illusions are shattered. They have been found out.

I live on a dark and clouded island. Around me are enchanting calls to forget the invisible and plunge into an exciting world of popularity, lust, greed, and power. Sometimes I feel foolish as I cling to the faint hope that there is a larger world that counts for more while the games of war and greed are played around me, splattering me.

One day, though, the Creator will come again. Every knee shall bend before Him. If I have persevered and served Him as my Lord, I will welcome Him with joy. And I will live forever in the warmth of His presence. My hope will be rewarded.

9

It Hurts

I have never thought that a Christian would be free of suffering. For our Lord suffered. And I have come to believe that He suffered, not to save us from suffering, but to teach us how to bear suffering. For He knew that there is no life without suffering.

ALAN PATON
Cry, the Beloved Country

Thirteen years ago our family moved into a Chicago suburb raised up in what had been a cornfield only a year before. We chose one of the six models with individual features such as varied colors of plastic tile in the bathrooms. Most of our neighbors were people moving out from the city to escape multiple-family dwellings and to seek the joys and new freedoms their savings and hard work had provided.

Across the street from us was a house exactly like our own. The family that moved in, like ours, had three children. They were good neighbors. However, at this point, life's similarities end. Our first encounter with their tragedy came when their daughter's fiancé was killed in Vietnam. We prayed together and encouraged her to allow the wounds to heal. In about a year she hesitantly allowed herself to fall in love again, only to have this man die in an auto accident.

About the same time Art, her father, was severely burned while at work and spent nine agonizing months in the burn center of Cook County Hospital bravely fighting the various painful complications as well as the burns. Each day was filled with reports of hope, then crisis, then despair, then victory. Finally, when it seemed he had won, he suddenly took a turn for the worse and died. Now five years have passed and the oldest son is suffering from a seemingly incurable blood disorder and the youngest son has developed tumors in his eyes that at this point appear inoperable.

During this same period our family has experienced no serious illness. Our oldest daughter is preparing for college, and the other two are facing nothing more serious than whether they will make sports teams or how to deal with skin blemishes. What is the answer to these inequities? Before God I don't want our family to be any other way, but it is impossible for me to watch others without asking some serious questions and without facing no little agony.

I have opened Pandora's box. In the last chapter I showed why I believe God does indeed work in this world, combining the supernatural and natural. But I have entered a cloudier room—the room of suffering. If God does work in this world why doesn't He do a better job? Why so much blood and pain? Why are children's worlds so full of unexplained grief? This one fact of life slaps us every time we piously declare our faith. If anything is process, pain is process.

No explanation of suffering will suffice because the person in pain never wants an explanation. An explanation is theoretical, philosophical, removed. Rather, the suffering asker wants a solution. And that is the dilemma of pain. No one has the solution. We are left mumbling hollow truisms about a loving God and a fallen world.

I have no solutions. But I still have to face the mother of the seventeen-year-old who just smashed on a freeway and the father of the five-year-old he's just run over; so I have had to confront the problem. I present here a few principles that help me in grappling with this subject.

Any thoughts on pain must begin with our view of God. Because we live on a hostile planet, we tend to project our interpretation of reality onto God. We see jealousy, revenge, and cruelty, and we attach those qualities to our image of God. Primitive religions did so much more blatantly. The Scandinavians would send maidens out to sea in boats full of fruits and gifts to appease the gods. If the maidens never returned, the gods were pleased.

We are more subtle now, but we cannot help projecting some of our bitterness and frustration onto our God. It helps me to start, not by blaming God for the world, but by asking what His purpose is. The Christian faith tells us that God is wholly good. Thus, for an earth this fractured to exist, He must be trying something very strange. I can't believe that God is capricious and unjust; so I turn my attention on what He is doing in the world. I call what God is doing—the human project.

The universe is a rather spacious creation. Our own galaxy, which contains one hundred billion stars, is just one of a hundred billion such galaxies. Most scientists believe the universe is expanding outward at an incredible rate of speed, and this requires a delicate balance of rotation, pulsation, gravitation. Yet, somehow, everything stays in order. Big as it is, the universe seems to be functioning in perfect order, just as God planned.

If our earth exploded in a nuclear holocaust, the view from another galaxy would appear as a tiny match flaring for a second, then dying. For the rest of the universe, the event wouldn't even be visible. Yet, on this insignificant speck, something astoundingly rebellious is happening. Two-legged creatures in great numbers, defying the laws of the universe, are standing up and saying to God, "Leave me alone. I will determine my life, and I don't need Your advice!" Even more astounding, God listens. He respects us enough to let us rebel.

By creating beings with free wills, omnipotent God submitted to the possibility of such rebellion. Is that defeat? C. S. Lewis replies, "What you call defeat, I call miracle; for to make things which are not Itself, and thus to become, in a sense, capable of being resisted by its own handiwork, is the most astonishing and unimaginable of all the feats we attribute to the Deity."

Many people tend to think of God as playing in one of the Japanese puppet shows as the puppeteer who dresses in black but is just visible and works openly against a black backdrop—a subtle reminder to viewers that the puppets are not their own masters. But, in the human project, God limited Himself. He gave the puppets a will, and dropped the strings. Man chose against Him, and sin and suffering thus entered our planet.

Could God have done it another way? I ask myself that every time a heartbroken parent comes to me and spills out his soul and every time I come down with an irritating sore throat or virus that interrupts my plans.

To answer, I'd need another book, a lifetime of study, and revelation no man has ever been given. The best clear explanation I've found is in C. S. Lewis's *The Problem of Pain*. Among a host of brilliant arguments, he makes one strong point. Pain tells us something is wrong. The entire human condition is out of whack. We are a rebel fortress; we are cursed, and every sting and ache reminds us.

It's true of physical pain. The nervous system is a marvelously complex electronic design. A mountain climber, feeling the tugs and ripples of a rope, can gauge precisely every action of his partner a hundred feet below. This marvelous nervous system seems to revolt if something is wrong. Short-circuiting all our brain's activities, pain screams at us, "Fix me. I need attention. Something strange has happened."

It's true in the moral realm also. Without pain, we would contentedly build our kingdom of self-sufficiency and pride, professing not to need God. (Didn't Adam?) Pain removes that privilege. It proves to us that reality is not the way it was meant to be. Something is wrong with a life of wars, screams, and insults. We need help.

At one time I thought that a sick person was unspiritual, that Christians didn't need God's megaphone. I thought that if I prayed, a tornado bearing down on my house would magically lift and hop over to the houses of pagans. But we know that doesn't happen. We live in a tainted world. Nothing in Scripture hints that we should expect it to be easier, more antiseptic, safer. My role is to cling to Him despite the world of pain (and sometimes because of it).

I think back to the hospital hallways and intensive-care rooms I've been in. Something about an intensive-care situation strips us of all our masks. We are at ground zero. Nothing else is important. Blue collar, white collar, black, white, male, female—those status games don't matter in intensive care. What matters is life and death. Pain and only pain can shout loud enough to bring us to that point.

I once participated in a funeral service for a teenage boy who was killed in a car accident. His mother tried to comfort us all: "The Lord took him home. He must have had some purpose. Thank You, Lord." Hearing her sob and grit her teeth, trying to accept a God who would do that, upset me so much that I could hardly keep silent. I wanted to ask

her, "Do you really think God reached down, picked up
your son's car, and dropped it smack in front of that oncom-
ing car?" What actually happened was that a drunk dozed
off, and his car slid across the median, directly into the path
of her son's car. It was tragic, but it was the result of existing natural conditions, and if I set up those same conditions,
the accident would probably occur again.

Most of the mental turmoil about pain and suffering
hinges on this issue: Who's causing it? Is God a sadist,
delighting in watching me squirm? The Bible does record
certain instances where the direct cause of suffering is
clear. For example, Jesus declared in Luke 13:16 that Satan
kept a woman bound in disease for eighteen years. God
Himself directly caused pain in the Old Testament, such as
in the plagues on Egypt. But most of the time, the Bible
specifically sidesteps the question of cause.

Job, of course, is the classic treatment of suffering. Job
and his friends weighed every possible reason for his suffering but came up with no solution. When God did intervene,
though, He did a very peculiar thing. He gave Job a lecture
about wild animals and oddities of nature. He overwhelmed
Job with His greatness and the question of cause completely faded from Job's mind. He fell to his knees and
repented.

In the same chapter referred to earlier, Luke 13, Jesus in
another instance pushed the question of causality away
from His listeners. Someone informed Him of an
atrocity—Pilate had butchered Jews as they were sacrific-
ing in the temple. Jesus turned and said, "Do you think they
were worse sinners than other men from Galilee?" He
brought up another tragedy—the death of eighteen men
when the Tower of Siloam fell—and asked the same question. In each case He followed up with a ringing warning:
"Don't you realize that you also will perish unless you
leave your evil ways and turn to God?" Thus, He declared,
these instances of suffering were not a result of the people's

actions. Instead, He focused on the people's response. Pain and death are a warning to us that something is dreadfully wrong. We will perish if we do not repent.

Paul's epistles bear the same note. Whether the suffering was from persecution by enemies or his "thorn in the flesh," he emphasized the response of acceptance and faithfulness. God demands our faithfulness in the midst of tribulation. If we endure, we will be rewarded.

Hebrews 11 records a roll call of the faithful, including many victories attained, kingdoms won, dangers escaped. But right along with the success stories are those beaten to death, whipped, chained, stoned, starved in the desert. They are described as ". . . hungry and sick and ill-treated—too good for this world. And these men of faith, though they trusted God and won his approval, none of them received all that God had promised them; for God wanted them to wait and share the even better rewards that were prepared for us" (Hebrews 11:38–40). Exactly! "Too good for this world"—so good that horrible pain did not sway them. And their faithfulness through it was not in vain; they were ultimately rewarded.

To those of us in the midst of the suffering, a future reward is scant comfort. But it is *some* comfort, at least, and these few years seen from the vista of eternity will probably change our perspectives.

I have a friend who struggled with the command: "In every thing give thanks . . ." (1 Thessalonians 5:18 KJV). He could obey it as long as life was bearable, not too extreme. But one day, as he was driving across the state to give his testimony at a church meeting, the pain got too much. He had a son with a learning disability, and it seemed at the time that all the good they'd ever done for this boy was backfiring. In addition, the man's business was failing badly, and he was having to cut employees and change his life-style. How could he thank God? The verse drilled over and over again in his mind, and at last he cried out, "God, it's impossible. It's too much to ask of a man."

As he poured out his heart to God, continuing along the

freeway, he worked it through until at last he had an answer. When he returned, he told me with great enthusiasm, "Jay, I've got it. The verse means, 'Thank You, God. You trust me to live in the real world, not in a protective incubator. I can give thanks for "everything" — for the whole scheme of things.' The fact is that good grows with evil, that patience comes through pain, and God trusts me enough to let me be a man, a free man."

Good grows along with the evil. My response in a situation can redeem it. I do not have to succumb to the pain and evil. Through Christ I can be victorious.

Hundreds of thousands of Christians have seen that truth in the life of Corrie ten

"Now, here's my plan . . ."

(*From* Now, Here's My Plan *by Shel Silverstein. Copyright © 1960 by Sheldon Silverstein. Reprinted by permission of Simon & Schuster, Inc., a division of Gulf & Western Corporation.*)

Boom, through her testimony and her book *The Hiding Place*. In the midst of the grossest possible human conditions inside a Nazi concentration camp, she triumphed. By giving thanks, surrendering to God, and concentrating on her response, not the cause, she triumphed.

No prayer is wasted; no hurt goes unheard. To the faithful, God is faithful, sometimes intervening, but always storing up our faithfulness for rewards.

I must admit that it's hard for me to accept pain as a part of the process of life. I want to banish it. But I've begun to think that this yearning for a tension-free world, full of pleasure alone, is a non-Christian idea. The Bible view shows Christians surviving in a hostile environment. We are to *expect* pain. It is a legitimate part of human experience which Christ Himself endured. On His last night on earth Christ predicted that His followers would encounter pain.

This fact struck me as I was conducting orientation sessions for members of a teenage musical team headed for Caracas, Venezuela. We had several weeks of training, and I began to listen to the prayers of these earnest young Christians. They said things such as, "Lord, I'm not perfect. I'm a sinner. Please make me the perfect ideal for those Venezuelans. Help me not to falter."

As I listened to the prayers, I sensed that these kids were repeatedly apologizing for their humanity. They genuinely hoped to find a pain-free, sin-free life. I thought of a sign I'd seen in some store offices: CUSTOMERS ARE NOT AN INTERFERENCE TO YOUR WORK, BUT A REASON FOR IT. It's also true that our humanity is not an interference to Christ's work, but the reason for it.

My role as a Christian is not to gouge out all pain and flaws—that's dead-end legalism. My job is to accept the forgiveness and grace of Christ and rely on it to sustain me through this hostile environment.

Pain demands response. In a time of stress, do we curse God and die or do we turn toward Him, not away from

Him? Peter said, "Lord, where else would we go?" (*see* John 6:68).

In situations such as waiting outside an intensive-care unit, I have learned to say, "Lord, I don't understand why, but where else could I go?" When I do turn toward Him, heed His megaphone, He meets me. He doesn't always take away the suffering. But when I do respond toward God, He does make all things work together for good.

The arguments about pain are bandied back and forth and are never fully resolved. In moments of doubt, none of them makes sense to me. But one thing I've found to be universally helpful is, thinking of the example of Jesus, the One who preceded us.

God came to earth. He saw, and felt, for Himself. Dorothy Sayers said in *Christian Letters to a Post-Christian World:*

> . . . for whatever reason God chose to make man as he is—limited and suffering and subject to sorrows and death—He had the honesty and the courage to take His own medicine. Whatever game He is playing with His creation, He has kept His own rules and played fair. He can exact nothing from man that He has not exacted from Himself. He has Himself gone through the whole of human experience, from the trivial irritations of family life and the cramping restrictions of hard work and lack of money to the worst horrors of pain and humiliation, defeat, despair, and death. When He was a man, He played the man. He was born in poverty and died in disgrace and thought it well worthwhile.

Jesus did not shun the curse of pain and suffering. It's the difference between the phone booth and the manger. Jesus was not a superman who changed into a human costume to hide His divinity. He was fully human. The bullets did not bounce off Him. Willingly, He took it on Himself, turning the curse of pain and death into our redemption.

We who live on planet Earth cannot easily comprehend God's plan for humans. We cannot view Jesus' coming from the perspective of the universe. J. B. Phillips, however, attempted to give us that viewpoint by imagining a conversation between two angels. Perhaps some of the marvel of the Visit can be seen in his fantasy.

Once a very young angel was being shown round the splendors and glories of the universe by a senior and experienced angel. To tell the truth, the little angel was beginning to be tired and a little bored. He had been shown whirling galaxies and blazing suns, infinite distances in the deathly cold of the interstellar space, and to his mind there seemed to be an awful lot of it all. Finally he was shown the galaxy of which our planetary system is but a small part. As the two of them drew near to the star which we call our sun and to its circling planets, the senior angel pointed to a small and rather insignificant sphere turning very slowly on its axis. It looked as dull as a dirty tennis ball to the little angel, whose mind was filled with the size and glory of what he had seen.

"I want you to watch that one particularly," said the senior angel, pointing with his finger.

"Well, it looks very small and rather dirty to me," said the little angel. "What's special about that one?"

"That," replied his senior, "is the Visited Planet."

"Visited? You don't mean visited by . . . ?"

"Indeed I do. That ball has been visited by our young Prince of Glory." And he bowed his head reverently.

"But how?" queried the younger one. "Do you mean that our great and glorious Prince, with all these wonders and splendors of His Creation, and millions more that I'm sure I haven't seen yet, went down in Person to this fifth-rate little ball? Why should He do a thing like that?"

"It isn't for us," said his senior a little stiffly, "to question His 'why's,' except that He is not impressed by size and numbers, as you seem to be. As to why He became one of them—how else do you suppose He could visit them?"

The little angel's face wrinkled in disgust.

"Do you mean to tell me," he said, "that He stooped so low as to become one of those creeping, crawling creatures of that floating ball?"

"I do, and I don't think He would like you to call them 'creeping, crawling creatures' in that tone of voice. For, strange as it may seem to us, He loves them. He went down to visit them to lift them up to become like Him."

The little angel looked blank. Such a thought was almost beyond his comprehension.

"Close your eyes for a moment," said the senior angel, "and we will go back in what they call time."

While the little angel's eyes were closed and the two of them moved nearer to the spinning ball, it stopped its spinning, spun backwards quite fast for a while, and then slowly resumed its usual rotation.

"Now look!" And there appeared here and there on the dull surface of the globe little flashes of light, some merely momentary and some persisting for quite a time.

"You are watching this little world as it was some thousands of years ago," said the senior angel. "Every flash and glow of light that you see is something of the Father's knowledge and wisdom breaking into the minds and hearts of people who live upon the earth. Not many people, you see, can hear His Voice or understand what He says, even though He is speaking gently and quietly to them all the time."

"Why are they so blind and deaf and stupid?" asked the junior angel rather crossly.

"It is not for us to judge them. We who live in the

Splendor have no idea what it is like to live in the dark. We hear the music and the Voice like the sound of many waters every day of our lives, but to them—well, there is much darkness and much noise and much distraction upon the earth. Only a few who are quiet and humble and wise hear His Voice. But watch, for in a moment you will see something truly wonderful.''

The Earth went on turning and circling round the sun, and then quite suddenly, in the upper half of the globe, there appeared a light, tiny but so bright in its intensity that both the angels hid their eyes.

"I think I can guess," said the little angel in a low voice. "That was the Visit, wasn't it?"

"Yes, that was the Visit. The Light Himself went down there and lived among them. But in a moment, the light will go out."

"But why? Could He not bear their darkness and stupidity? Did He have to return here?"

"No, it wasn't that," returned the senior angel. His voice was stern and sad. "They failed to recognize Him for Who He was—or at least only a handful knew Him. For the most part they preferred their darkness to His light, and in the end they killed Him."

"The fools, the crazy fools! They don't deserve . . . ."

"Neither you nor I, nor any other angel, knows why they were so foolish and so wicked. Nor can we say what they deserve or don't deserve. But the fact remains, they killed our Prince of Glory while He was Man."

"And that I suppose was the end? I see the whole Earth has gone black and dark."

"Wait, we are still far from the end of the story of the Visited Planet. Watch now, but be ready to cover your eyes again."

In utter blackness the earth turned round three

times, and then there blazed with unbearable radiance a point of light.

"What now?" asked the little angel, shielding his eyes.

"They killed Him all right, but He conquered death. The thing most of them dread and fear all their lives He broke and conquered. He rose again, and a few of them saw Him and from then on became His utterly devoted slaves."

"Thank God for that," said the little angel.

"Amen. Open your eyes now, the dazzling light has gone. The Prince has returned to His Home of Light. But watch the Earth now."

As they looked, in place of the dazzling light there was a bright glow which throbbed and pulsated. And then as the Earth turned many times little points of light spread out. A few flickered and died, but for the most part the lights burned steadily, and as they continued to watch, in many parts of the globe there was a glow over many areas.

"You see what is happening?" asked the senior angel. "The bright glow is the company of loyal men and women He left behind, and with His help, they spread the glow, and now lights begin to shine all over the Earth."

"Yes, yes," said the little angel impatiently, "but how does it end? Will the little lights join up with each other? Will it all be light, as it is in Heaven?"

His senior shook his head. "We simply do not know," he replied. "It is in the Father's hands. Sometimes it is agony to watch, and sometimes it is joy unspeakable. The end is not yet. But now I am sure you can see why this little ball is so important. He has visited it; He is working out His Plan upon it."

"Yes, I see, though I don't understand. I shall never forget that this is the Visited Planet."

10

The Sin of Sodom

. . . Sodom's sins were pride and laziness and too much food, while the poor and needy suffered outside her door.

Ezekiel 16:49

Zacek

(Zdenek Zacek)

To the American nostril, the smell was completely foreign. If you blindfolded me, put me in a plane, and it touched down in India, I think I could tell you, before the door opened, where I was again.

Odor from poor sanitation mixed with the spices and the heat to create a most oppressive climate. This was during the late sixties—my first visit to any country of great poverty.

That night I walked with a friend through the city of Hyderabad. It shocked me to see so many people on the streets. They lay on the pavements, even sprawled on the airport runway to sleep against its warmth. We walked slowly, letting the impact soak in. Once we saw a dog, emaciated and shrunken to the shape of his bones, barely totter down the street. He stopped, wavered for a few seconds, then fell over dead. Under a streetlight, I watched a lady sweep the gutter with her hand and comb through the filth for a matchbox, something of value, or perhaps a morsel to eat.

As we turned a corner near the hotel, we found ourselves on one street that seemed deserted. Everything was silent, and I glanced nervously behind me, unused to the stillness. Soon we started hearing a regular thumping—followed by a dragging, scraping sound. Thump, scrape, thump, scrape. It was a beggar—a young boy with no legs. His tiny crutches barely reached his armpits, and he used them to drag the trunk of his body along the street. I stood motionless, watching in pity and horror, until I realized he was coming toward us. He asked for alms, and I reached in my pocket and handed him all the coins I had. He thanked me and dragged himself away.

We had turned toward the hotel and were several yards away when we heard a sudden commotion. Other beggars had appeared from nowhere and were crowding around this legless boy, beating him with his crutches, kicking him, and stealing the coins. The fracas was loud, but it lasted only a few seconds, and then all the others disappeared. Left in a crumpled heap in the street was the young boy with his crutches.

I did not sleep the rest of that night. Images of what I had seen kept flashing before me. I felt weighted, heavy, and yet frightened, like a child who has just stood next to railroad tracks while a huge locomotive whooshed by. The problems of the world were so big, so vast. Yes, I had seen the beggars and the street sleepers in photos and on TV. But those two-dimensional images had never jumped into real-

ity for me until that moment. I thought of my own puny
egotism. I had thrown my body against the world and, with
my preaching and praying, expected to change it all by
myself.

The world, I discovered, was far, far bigger than I. All
my frenzied efforts to change it would at most make a
scarcely noticeable dent, or could backfire, like the scene
that night. I never recovered from that initial shock on that
trip through Asia. Live bodies were everywhere. Driving
through the streets was like plowing snow. Somehow the
mass of humans would bend just enough to let cars through.

When I returned to America, I began to see that perhaps
"the great blessings of America" flowed because our
forefathers happened to land on a continent with rivers,
trees, and good soil. I had seen some of the great rivers of
the world which cause destructive floods during the rainy
season and become puny streams the rest of the year. I
realized that my pity for the third world had been based on
my superior attitude—if they did things my way, the
American way, it might be different for suffering people.
Not so. Their condition is so complex and difficult that I
began to despair of all solutions.

I felt differently about my faith also. Would all the
world's problems be solved if everyone I preached to accepted Jesus Christ? I saw that the problem is bigger than
men or any individual effort—it needs all of us working
together.

About A.D. 125 a philosopher, Saint Aristides, delivered
to Emperor Hadrian of Rome a defense of the faith which
included this description of Christians:

> They love one another; the widow's needs are not ig-
> nored, and they rescue the orphan from the person who
> does him violence. He who has gives to him who has
> not, ungrudgingly and without boasting . . . . If they
> find poverty in their midst and they do not have spare

food, they fast two or three days in order that the needy might be supplied with necessities.

Could that description be written today?

During another trip I stopped off in a white-dominated part of Africa. While there, I spent some time with a fine Christian who lived on an estate in the rolling hill country. One afternoon he took us to the hills behind his estate and showed his guests a clever sport. It involves superb horsemanship. A rider carrying a spear approaches a tiny dangling ring at a full gallop and thrusts his spear through the ring. We were all pleasantly entertained by his skill and spent the afternoon enjoying the beauty of the countryside. Poverty, racism, and politics seemed far away.

Then across the hills, we could see a tiny figure stirring up dust as he sprinted toward us. We watched him for several minutes as our host explained he was probably one of his black houseboys.

The black youth arrived, panting and sweating, bowed, and handed our host a note. He took it, read it, then turned livid. In a crisp, hard tone, he told us the prime minister of South Africa had just been assassinated. Gentlemanliness vanished as this man turned on his houseboy. "What your country doesn't realize," he said over his shoulder to us, "is that kaffirs (equivalent to *niggers*) are afraid of the knife and spear. They're from the jungle. You need to equip your police with knives, not guns, if you want to keep these kaffirs under control."

Still on the horse, he began threatening the frightened houseboy with the spear. The boy's eyes widened in terror, and he backed off, then turned and ran toward the house. Though he probably intended no harm, my host's cruel joke startled me. I had to rebuke him for scaring the youth.

When I argued with this man, he brought up facts about American blacks and American Indians that I had never heard. He documented massacres and lynchings from American history. "We keep them under control," he said, "but at least we haven't killed them off, like you did to the Indians." I was painfully struck with my own use of racial humor and stereotyping.

The dual impact of seeing such physical needs and moral injustices has never left me. It made me commit myself to a lifetime struggle for human rights as a part of my faith. I realized I had to get involved in a corporate way, applying Christ's principles to social issues.

The call is not a new one. Evangelical publications have lifted up the banner of social concern, and information on what to do is readily available. Still, I sense a fear of involvement among many. Instead of being the salt of the earth as Jesus commanded, sometimes we're on display in a hermetically sealed salt jar—a mere curiosity.

Apathy is a natural tendency I have to fight constantly. I tend to want an antiseptic life, and in the suburbs we can forget the extremes of life—pain, deprivation. It's easy to forget those starving faces are humans, God's valuable handiwork.

Most of the country has long abandoned the moral crusades of the sixties. Apathy reigns even on college campuses, not so much because students don't care, but because they think they can't make a difference. We're caught up in more personal issues or in domestic ones such as inflation. How many cries do you hear for increased foreign aid?

It's not just an overseas problem. Even in America the evangelical church has skirted the concerns of a large part of the population—the blue-collar working class and the poor. My dad used to complain about preachers. He tried a number of churches where the pulpit illustrations described going to the office, eating in restaurants, flying on planes. "What's the matter with preachers?" he'd say. "Don't any of them ride buses or eat out of lunch boxes or work with their hands? Does *anybody* in the church?" We are painted as the comfortable status quo of society that refuses to be touched with social needs. If an evangelical church does carve out a dynamic inner-city ministry, it's publicized as a remarkable exception in all our magazines. Consider this in view of Christ's stinging commands to feed the hungry, heal the sick, and give to the impoverished. What's happened?

At times, I despair of solutions. Yet, as I study history, I become more and more convinced that though we can't usher in a utopia, we can do a lot better than our current record. In eighteenth-century England, for example, it looked as though the social structure was crumbling. A slave ship called the *Good Ship Jesus* plied waters to the New World, symbolizing the type of "justice" supported by most Christians. *Cambridge Modern History* sums up the time as one of "expiring hopes." England seemed on the verge of a bloodbath like that of France, until John Wesley's Evangelical Awakening hit like a monsoon wind. In a few decades the tide turned.

Historian J. Wesley Bready traces the awakening and its effects which surged through individuals into the factory, the marketplace, and the seats of learning and government. He says:

> The early leaders were pre-eminently ambassadors of Christ who had experienced in their own lives the transforming power of the Gospel, and though not indifferent to social and political affairs, they felt the "call" to preach a Gospel which transforms men rather than to agitate for social reconstruction. Indeed had Wesley and Whitefield spent their careers as social reformers they would have lived disillusioned lives, and died heartbroken men. From their efforts, however, emerged the most profound political and social achievements, thus illustrating history's central truth: that the changing of the hearts of men is ever the surest road toward lifting the level of human society.

There are signs of similar fresh winds among evangelicals today. But I can find no concerted effort among us. I see a few communes and "intentional communities" which slice off a small segment of problems to deal with. And I see a few Christian politicians such as Senator Mark Hatfield, Representative John Anderson, and Arthur Simon, president of Bread for the World. But even Senator Hatfield gets most of his hate mail from Christians who condemn him for his stances on social issues and on war. (See his book *Between a Rock and a Hard Place*.) Often Christians I meet seem content to let the world manage itself, while they seek personal happiness.

Underneath those of us from fundamentalist backgrounds, there still lurks a suspicion of any appeal not directed specifically to the individual. We can understand appeals for prayer or for money, but concerted political action—that smacks of the dreaded "social Gospel" days.

After seeing the realities of the world, I know I can't do it on my own. None of us can. We need individual commitment, but also an organized, comprehensive approach.

I tire quickly of the preachments I hear about the starving world. The statistics on the African famines, the million new Indian babies born each month, and all those malnourished children blur together. I want the problems to go away; I want to forget. But I can't.

I can't because I think back to the thin, expressionless face of the legless beggar I met in India. If he came to my doorstep in West Chicago, I would be moved to tears and expend a whirlwind of energy to feed, clothe, and give him the medical care he needs. If he lived ten miles away, and I knew about him, I'd do the same. Do I have the right, then, to make him suffer because he happens to live ten thousand miles away?

Again, there is no clear answer for the Christian. Every decision I make to find self-fulfillment and happiness for myself and my family must come against the background of a world struggling for survival, not fulfillment. I have to pray before God, asking Him to direct me in sorting out His goals for my life. In the same way, Jesus narrowed the whole world's need to focus on a relatively few people, who could go out into the world and make real changes. I cannot do it myself, but neither can I give up. If we Christians don't bring God's love and healing power to a bleeding world, who will?

The well-known passage, Matthew 25:40, which ends, ". . . Inasmuch as ye have done it unto one of the least of these my brethren, ye have done it unto me" (KJV), haunts me. That verse revolutionized the life of a Roman soldier, Martin of Tours, who became a missionary bishop. He changed vocations because of an experience he had helping a beggar in Amiens on a cold winter day. Having no money to give the shivering man, he took off his frayed military cloak, cut it in two, and gave half to the beggar.

That night Martin had a dream in which he saw angels, encircling Jesus, who was wearing half of a Roman soldier's coat. An angel asked, "Master, why are You wearing that worn old cloak? Who gave it to You?" Jesus answered, "My servant Martin gave it to Me."

Too often my mental picture of Jesus is of a compassionate helper who ministers to the poor and needy. But as this verse shows, Jesus stands on the side of the poor. By ministering to them, we are in fact ministering to Christ Himself. There is no place for paternalism and pity when I think of Christian service in that light.

11

The Christian Look

Ideas are poor ghosts until they become specific in another person; then they reach out to us with fiery hands and shake us like a passion.

GEORGE ELIOT

What does a Christian look like? Many times I have sheepishly discovered what he shouldn't look like. He shouldn't be so frantically busy that he leaves no room for compassion. He shouldn't be a starchy legalist with long lists of self-righteous rules. He shouldn't expect a life void of pain and suffering. And he's not required to be offensively frontal with the Gospel, plastering his car with bumper stickers and wearing a Jesus sweatshirt.

Those extremes are the stages I've gone through. They have been my process. Unfortunately, I have not been alone in giving the world a false impression of what a Christian should look like. If you ask the average person on the street what an evangelical Christian is, he'll probably describe something close to an ethnic culture, not a theology. He may think of a Christian college nearby where kids wear short hair, don't smoke, and don't push in cafeteria lines. To many people, evangelical Christianity is a harmless curiosity. It doesn't compel people to reevaluate themselves. Most don't see the healing salve of the Gospel which can be applied to ragged marriages, fits of depression, and the tearing competition of the business world.

Defining a Christian is a slippery business. We don't attract stares in airports like the Hare Krishna people with their saffron robes and strange hairstyles. We don't face east five times a day and bow in prayer like the Moslems. To complicate matters, almost every group of Christians has its own description of the ideal Christian.

I have spent much time stumbling around, diving headfirst down avenues of the Christian life which turned out to be dead ends. I'm finally learning what a Christian should not be. But what should he be?

The pages of the New Testament rustle with the command to stand out from the world. A Christian must be different *somehow*.

As I read the Bible one day, suddenly I rediscovered in Galatians 5:22 a list of words called the fruits of the Spirit. The qualities Paul rattles off describe what should result when a person is truly indwelled by the Holy Spirit of God. These characteristics spring up when Christ is present.

Love

Not far away in Paul's writings is a complete definition of this fruit. The love chapter, 1 Corinthians 13, spells it out in realistic detail. And the quality of love in that chapter differs remarkably from our preconceptions. Influenced by valentines, Gothic romances, and TV, we tend to think of love as sugary, painless, romantic.

The love Paul describes is hard work. It is patient and kind, never envious or jealous, never boastful or proud, never haughty, selfish, or rude. It does not demand its own way, is not irritable or touchy, does not hold grudges and will hardly even notice when others do it wrong. If I love someone, I'll love him no matter what, Paul says.

Love this complete is hard to visualize. I need to see it fleshed out in a person, and the model which has helped me best is the natural love shown by that great invention called mothers. Something about a mother's love is bedrock per-

manent. She's the first to respond with help if her child runs
into a crisis. Even if the child is totally undeserving, a
mother continues loving loyally. She never resents her
child's success. She delights in it. She sees her child's mature growth as the end result and sacrifices herself totally to
make that happen. It's an incredible thing, a mother's love,
and anyone who's felt it knows immediately what I mean.

Imagine for a moment a person with that same thick,
stubborn love directed toward all his friends and neighbors.
He would tenaciously help tackle their problems and rejoice
victoriously in their successes. He would care as deeply
about their egos as he does about his own. If you see a
person like that, who shows love not just toward people
who love him back but to the wayward and the needy,
chances are he may be a Christian.

Mother's love comes naturally enough to mothers; after
all, they see their children as extensions of themselves. A
steady, consistent love toward the unlovable must come
from God. It's one of His fruits, the sign of His presence.

C. S. Lewis preached a sermon in 1941 which since has
been printed in his book *The Weight of Glory*. He begins by
saying that if you ask twenty good men today what they
thought to be the highest of the virtues, nineteen of them
would reply, "unselfishness." But, he continues, if you
asked almost any of the great Christians of old, they would
have replied, "love." A negative term has been substituted
for a positive one. One is a self-denial for the sake of self-
denial, the other is motivated by an ultimate concern for
another person.

Lewis ends his sermon by describing the explosive power
of love of our neighbor:

> It is a serious thing to live in a society of possible gods
> and goddesses, to remember that the dullest and most
> uninteresting person you talk to may one day be a crea-
> ture which, if you saw it now, you would be strongly

tempted to worship, or else a horror and a corruption such as you now meet, if at all, only in a nightmare. All day long we are, in some degree, helping each other to one or the other of these destinations. It is in the light of these overwhelming possibilities, it is with the awe and the circumspection proper to them, that we should conduct all our dealings with one another, all friendships, all loves, all play, all politics. There are no *ordinary* people . . . .

Love is the language the Spirit provides to communicate to another person that we recognize his worth as a creation of God. This kind of sacrificial love can be humiliating, risky, emotionally draining—and incredibly rewarding. Love is not merely something we *feel*; it is something we do.

Joy

During certain periods of my life, I've had to search diligently to find the quality of joy among myself and my Christian friends. I have seen too many tight-lipped, intense, burdened Christians. It was once rare to find one with a relaxed sense of humor, a carefree spirit. Slowly this seems to be changing, but some still insist that spirituality and solemnity must go hand in hand.

For many years I had the attitude that a person in the midst of struggle and the growth process could not experience Christian joy. It belonged to a mystical "life on the highest plane" which I "someday" would reach, after God and I had solved all my problems. God has recently been teaching me joy is not a sealed, separate category of life which I can enter into when everything is calm and pain free.

It took me a while, but I finally learned that all my problems were not going to be solved in this life. God does not free us from struggle and process—often He delivers more of it. But He does give us this invigorating, infusing quality of joy.

Sometimes I have strayed off in the other direction and tried to make joy the goal of my Christian life. I have *worked* at being joyful. I can sense this tendency in many young Christians. If you attend a testimony meeting among teenagers, chances are you'll hear words such as these: "If you become a Christian, you'll be so happy!"; "God just filled me up with joy when I accepted Him."

I don't doubt those kids' experiences. But I think that sometimes they portray joy as a goal of the Christian life, rather than as a by-product. I think it's very significant that Paul uses the metaphor of fruit in describing these qualities. Joy is not a product you make like a model airplane, putting tab A into slot A. It is fruit—the by-product of fertilizer, sun, rain, and the health of the branch to which it's attached.

I have found that when I strive for joy, I don't get it. It creeps up on me unexpectedly, almost as a bonus God throws in to reward me. For example, there's a wonderful by-product of two Christians sharing love—fellowship. Often, if I am concentrating and praying for a brother and working on my love for him, joy will come. Or when I repel a temptation to sin and follow Jesus, joy will come.

Sister Theresa stands out as an example of this aspect of joy. If you've ever seen her on TV, you know the impact of her radiant joy. If you flipped channels on your TV and suddenly came upon the image of Sister Theresa, you would probably think, *Now there's a person who's found a comfortable, well-balanced life. Maybe if I listen, she'll tell me how to arrange my life so that I'll have more leisure time and more self-actualization.*

Actually, of course, Sister Theresa spends her days in one of the most depressing environments on earth—the slums of Calcutta. I have already described the filth and stench of parts of India. Sister Theresa deliberately goes

into the worst parts of the worst cities, finds those in the
gutters near death, and gently carries them to her hospital.
There, she and her staff lavish on those dying men, women,
and children the utmost care. They bathe them, bandage
their sores, fill them with nourishing food. They hold them
(many have never been held since they were babies). Sister
Theresa and her staff hug these people close to them and
show them love.

Most of Sister Theresa's patients don't make it. They
were too far gone when she found them. You see, she
specializes in the dying ones. An incredulous reporter once
asked her, "Sister, why do you waste your time on the
dying ones? You could find less miserable people who also
need help and do them more good, but the ones you choose
are usually beyond hope."

Sister Theresa stared at the reporter as if she could not
comprehend such a question. Then, in a soft voice, she
said, "Sir, all their lives these people have lived like dogs.
Don't they have the right to die like angels?"

Sister Theresa has found the key to joy—being an obe-
dient servant. Joy is the kiss of God's approval.

The sense of joy is not a feeling that everything is all right
here, that we belong. Rather, the New Testament shouts
with a sense of joyful tension. We have God already; yet
not quite. We have entered the Kingdom of God; yet we
wait for it expectantly. We have been forgiven, yet we repent. We have tasted; yet we wait to taste fully.

Peace

The quality of peace is very dear to me. Of all the fruits of
the Spirit, I think this one most aptly strikes at the difference Christ has made in my life. The more I am aware of
His presence, the more I have peace. He provides a resting
place where I can pause from the battle and allow my
wounds to heal.

I began to experience peace in the Christian sense only

when I realized that my lack of peace stemmed from my fear of God. There is a right way to fear God—with a sense of awe, reverence, and submission. But I feared God in a wrong way, as symbolized by my lack of trust. I feared that He would put me in impossible situations, that He would make me do undesirable chores, that He might take away my few pleasures in life. I didn't trust God's love.

Before my commitment to God's working in me through process, I frantically tried to patch up every problem area that came along. But in doing so I discovered that the degree to which I thought I had all my problems solved was the degree to which I had no peace. My dogmatism sprang from my insecurities and fears. When God broke through to me to the point that I could say, "No, I don't have all the answers, but I will trust God anyway," then the peace of God entered my life.

A man of faith does not run around trying to patch up his beliefs every time there's a leak in the dike. He doesn't get all excited when *Time* runs a cover story entitled "Is God dead?" or scientists discover a new fossil. Christ is the tiger, not us. It's not our duty to protect Him; He is here to protect us.

When I have God's peace, I don't walk around burdened, carrying my sins (or my children's shortcomings) on my shoulders. I am aware of God's cleansing, erasing forgiveness which takes the permanence of my shortcomings away. The Good News is that I have been freed and forgiven, and the Holy Spirit delights in bringing me that spirit of freedom.

When I'm in tune with God, it seems like being in an airplane on signal. I hear a steady hum of beep-beep-beeps. I'm on course. When I stray, the silence shocks me into realizing it. His voice is stilled when I choose to disobey it.

The peace of Christ thus gives me freedom to act boldly, daringly. If I am in tune with Him, I can step out and take risks for Him. When I fail, that same peace offers me comfort and solace.

Once I went into a surgeon's office which had an insignia with a Latin slogan as a wall decoration. I asked what it meant. He told me the story of how some medieval lord had asked all his advisors to come up with a slogan that would hold true in any crisis. Their slogan: "This too will pass."

A fellow Christian had given the surgeon this insignia during a tragic week when five of his patients had died. The slogan reminded him of the peace God can offer during our hardest times of tribulation, and he's kept it on his office wall ever since.

Only with Christ's forgiveness can we say about anything, "This too will pass."

Patience

Everything about my personality fights against the idea of patience. I want to win the world by myself, to see how long I can go without sleep so I can add one more brick to God's Kingdom.

Yet God has implanted evidence of the importance of patience all around me. Consider the seventeen-year locust. It starts ten inches below the ground and gradually makes its way through the top in different stages of growth. Every seventeen years the air sings with the vibrations of these insects. They last a few days, then die. No American would have thought of something so impractical!

Or, consider the way God worked in the Old Testament. He endured waves of repeated failures and rebellions by the Israelites. He protected the messianic line through centuries, all in preparation for the coming of His Son.

In her personal celebration of nature, the book *Pilgrim at Tinker Creek*, Annie Dillard described a scene that took place in her fifth-grade classroom. In January a teacher brought in a dull brown cocoon attached to an oak leaf. She then showed the class pictures of what was inside—a polyphemus moth. With a wingspread of six inches, the polyphemus moth is one of the few huge American silk moths, much larger than a giant swallowtail butterfly. Its wings are a velvet texture of brown, edged in bands of blue and pink. A startling eyespot, melding from deep blue to translucent yellow, adorns each wing. The children examined the picture of the moth in awe and then turned to examine the cocoon.

As the children passed around the cocoon, squeezing it in their hot little fists, the moth began to stir prematurely. Delighted, they wrapped it tighter and felt the pupa jerk violently. After much passing around of the moth and many squeals of delight, the teacher intervened and put the cocoon, still heaving and banging, into a mason jar. There was no stopping it. It was coming out, January or not. One end of the cocoon dampened, and then spread apart.

The moth emerged, fat and shaggy, a sodden crumple. He couldn't spread his wings. They were not ready. They hung, coated with a chemicallike varnish. "Those huge wings," Annie remembers, "stuck on his back in a torture of random pleats and folds, wrinkled as a dirty tissue, rigid as leather. They made a single nightmare clump still wracked with useless, frantic convulsions."

What happened? The moth was forced out before it was ready. If you assist a moth from a cocoon, or a bird from an egg, you endanger its life. The incubation time and thrashings of birth are necessary for growth and strength. By interrupting the process, you may unwittingly create a deformed monster.

Too often, I try to help moths out of cocoons. I want to do God's work for Him. When kids come in for counseling, I want to tell them exactly how to live their lives, rejecting them when they fail, allowing no tolerance for the gradual unfolding of wings. When a person seems near to accepting Christ, I want to force him to pray, even against his will.

But that is not God's way. His way is patience. The proof

is the incredible patience He demonstrates in the process of making me in His image. That patience I can get only from Him.

Kindness

The old virtue of kindness has gotten bad press recently. When you say the word to many people, they think of a doting grandfather or a backboneless Santa Claus. Fathers seldom urge their sons to "be kind." It's considered a feminine trait that just doesn't belong in the jarring world.

In contrast, Jesus' kindness was aimed directly at what was best for the person He was dealing with. Kindness toward the rich young ruler meant he had to confront the rat race of his life and consider a new set of values. Kindness to Peter meant a public rebuke. So I have come to believe kindness is the attitude I can have toward people which will best lead toward their maturity. Kindness to my children does not require that I give them candy and presents on demand. Kindness to the oppressed may not mean giving them my used clothes and beat-up furniture in a patronizing way. Kindness thinks of the recipient, not the giver.

The environment that I've found hardest to apply kindness in is the business world. Often in large companies, the emphasis on status and rank tends to build up walls between people. People on different levels aren't supposed to socialize with each other. A boss relates to his employee as his inferior. A Christian showing the fruit of kindness should stand out in a company like that.

That doesn't mean kindness will interfere with good business sense. The kindest action to take toward an employee may be to fire him, if he's wasting his life, unmotivated by a certain job. The kindest way to treat a boss may be to carefully confront him on issues.

Kindness has teeth in it. Like love, it makes us squirm

when we try it in life situations. It pierces through the artificial barriers we tend to create: man, woman, high class, low class, boss, employee. It sees people behind the distinction.

How is it possible to have kindness for people in light of their differences in intelligence, personality, and status? People are not equal so how can I treat them all with kindness? Here's where the beautiful picture of the Body of Christ comes in. As Paul reminds us, can the hand say to the foot, "I am more important than you?" No, they both fulfill their separate functions, are both essential for the smooth functioning of the body.

The church janitor has as much worth as a person as the church pastor. He is simply fulfilling a different function in the Body. (How many janitors do you know who feel that way?)

What brings us together is not anything worthy in us. It is that we have the same Head. It is His banquet. We are merely the guests. We all serve the same Lord.

Goodness

It would be useless for me to try to summarize goodness in a few paragraphs. The Bible takes several hundred pages to give us an idea of what it entails. Basically, it means obeying in spite of moods, feelings, or rationalizations. The content of that obedience comes from Scripture and from the Holy Spirit's guidance.

What I didn't learn about goodness for so long, though, was the fact that it doesn't happen all at once. I needed to learn about scraped knees. The first time I tried to roller-skate, it looked so easy. Kids all around me were gliding poetically, hopping over sidewalk curbs, whirling in quick circles. If I could walk, I could roller-skate, I figured. So I talked a neighbor into letting me borrow his skates, made the necessary adjustments with his rusty key, and buckled them on. I nonchalantly stood up to hand him back his key,

"Tell me more about this Christianity of yours. I'm terribly interested." (© Punch (*Rothco*).)

and suddenly I saw my feet rolling straight out in front of my torso. My brain hadn't signaled for them to do that, but *whooooosh,* there they went! I instantly learned why some mothers tie pillows to the backs of kids who take up skating.

For the next several weeks I took turns choosing which knee I'd land on. By then I'd at least progressed to falling forward, not backward. My knees were scraped and bruised, flecked with asphalt, but I could skate!

When I became a Christian, I thought it would be like becoming a Dorothy Hamill on wheels overnight. I couldn't foresee any practicing or the horror of falling down. There would be only smooth forward motion.

This point seems so obvious, yet, somehow, we still haven't learned to allow for failure—at least, certain kinds of failure. Sure, someone can get up in church and tell how he *used* to drink and run around with women, until Christ helped him change it, but how many people do you know who will stand up and describe how their marriage is falling apart right now and needs help?

In most churches I've attended, everyone smiles and shakes hands and acts very pleasant and polite. Underneath, those people are often bleeding. I know because I've heard their kids tell me about the quarrels and fights. And I've heard the parents' despairing remarks about "those kids of mine." But I know only the outer edges of the waves. The parents don't open up. "Church isn't the place for that," they say. Well, if it isn't, what is?

I've also seen how some churches react when a member gets a divorce. Some species of sea gulls will react violently if you alter the appearance of one of the flock. If you tie a red string around the leg of one, the other birds will gang up and peck the strange one to death within minutes. I've seen churches do that to divorced women, unwed mothers, and members with a more liberal code of conduct.

How unlike Jesus' response to the harlot as told in John 8. When the harlot came with repentance, Jesus immediately, stunningly, absolved her guilt and sent her away. He refused to dwell on it. Rather, He lashed at the Pharisees around her, her accusers, to bring to the surface their repressed guilt. To me, that's the function of the Body of Christ. We must bind up the wounds of the needy, the fallen. We must never make them feel uniquely horrible, like the banded sea gull. And we must also dig deep and gouge out any repressed guilt.

I like this true story of acceptance. A pastor told his church, "I just can't accept all of the Gospel anymore. I'm confused, not sure what I believe." He resigned, but the church refused to accept the resignation. Instead, they told him to preach exactly what he did believe for one year and then decide how he felt. They embraced him in love.

All that year the pastor wavered. When he had doubts, he shared them openly. When he hit a breakthrough and had a surge of faith, he said so. An intense struggle with his faith lasted almost an entire year. At the end of that time he wrote the beautiful hymn "O Love That Wilt Not Let Me Go." His church had ministered to him in his failure.

I feel closest to God when I wake up in the middle of the night. It's dark and quiet, and I'm all alone. I listen, trying to focus my groggy brain back into consciousness, and wonder, "What's it all about, really? This Gospel I go around preaching—is it such Good News? Am I different from anyone else? Is life anything but a crazy, meaningless spin?" It's then that I cry out, "God! God!" and I am flooded with a sense of His presence. God never condemns me for falling down. That's the pain of growth. But goodness means not staying down.

Faithfulness

Everyone has his own favorite visual picture of the Christian life. I've heard many describe it as a Canaan of delicious fruit and perfect climate which we enjoy in quiet repose. Others take a view that it's like the suburbs. It chops off the extremes at both ends—the extreme joys and the horrid fears of life. It shields us from pain and makes every day a carbon copy of the one before.

Others describe it as a desert with a minumum of carefully placed oases. The image I've found most helpful, and which seems to fit the Bible's teaching best for me, is an urban image. The phrase "in the world but not of the world" at one time meant to me a person surrounded with a polypropylene space suit who walked down the streets without ever touching them. I don't think that's what the phrase means. I think it means getting right in the midst of that subway-jamming, elbow-jabbing, Alka Seltzer crowd to show them there is a model. Life can be lived on new terms, with newly created people. The complexities around us will not be resolved. We won't find the Utopia, the City of God here. But we can actively live in the world as residents of God's Kingdom.

There's another reason I like that urban metaphor. It shows that a lot of life is grueling and demanding. Go to a steelworker in Hammond, Indiana, and ask him about how fulfilled he is in his job. Some of these steelworkers love their work and take pride in it. But they glean that pride from the result of their labor—the stretched muscles, the smooth ingot, the boss's praise. They don't take grinning delight in every ring of the sledgehammer, every blast from the furnace.

I once thought the Christian life was a series of rainbow-colored flashes. Change, I imagined, took place under a starlit sky when the Holy Spirit would suddenly swoop down uninvited and begin doing miracles while I observed from the inside.

Those flash points come, and they come with incredible richness. But in between are a whole series of tenacious, grueling decisions that are made just because I believe. Often my faith contradicts how I feel at any certain point. It is a grasping. C. S. Lewis described it this way: "What God does for us, He does in us. The process of doing it will appear to me (and not falsely) to be the daily or hourly repeated exercises of my own will in renouncing this attitude; especially each morning, for it grows all over me like a new shell each night. Failures will be forgiven; it is acquiescence that is fatal, the permitted, regularized presence of an area in ourselves which we still claim for our own. We may never, this side of death, drive the invader out of our territory; but we must be in the resistance."

Being a Christian is a long series of times when a determination to be faithful is all that keeps me going.

Gentleness

If I spent my life in New York City, I think after a few years I would seriously question whether such a thing as gentleness existed! Something about the driving competition and the masses of people have almost banished gentleness from the streets. Taxi drivers and waitresses compete to be the gruffest, most harsh and irritating. Every group and minority has to march and shout for recognition.

Of course, I'm exaggerating. Gentleness must exist in New York, *somewhere*. If you spend some time there, though, I imagine you'll agree that gentleness is an expendable quality in our society. It seems to get squeezed out. And it takes a determined Christian to bring gentleness back to this earth.

Gentleness seems to me to be a little different from the

other fruits of the Spirit. It's not so much a *state* that describes how I am; it's a style of how I relate. I like to attach it to the quality of kindness. Kindness has as its goal the fulfillment or worth of the other person. Gentleness is the way in which I apply that kindness.

For example, I've mentioned that kindness may compel me to take a strong action, such as firing someone from a job. Gentleness is the style in which I communicate that to him. I don't have to bludgeon him or attack his self-image. I don't have to demonstrate my power and authority in a stern lecturing tone.

Gentleness seems to fit best in a person whose ego is not threatened by others. A gentle person doesn't have to flare up in competition or get back at someone vengefully. He is free to let his ego be stepped on without striking back.

A gentle father illustrates this quality best for me. A father may be a monstrous hunk of person—strong and practically invincible. But if he knows what gentleness is, he never threatens his kids with his size or strength. He conveys love to them tenderly.

Once again God fits the father analogy perfectly. Though omnipotent, He doesn't force or coerce. Someone once said to me, "Above all else, the Holy Spirit is a gentleman." And it's true. In the Bible, when the rich young ruler refused to accept Jesus' command to sell all he had and walked away, Jesus looked at him sadly and loved him anyway.

God loves us though He is complete without our love, or even our existence. He does not overwhelm us. Sometimes He is so gentle that we tend to overlook Him or even scorn Him. But even that doesn't threaten God. It grieves Him.

Self-control

For a long time in my Christian life, I confused the concept of self-control with self-reliance. I had my list of rules on what a Christian should and should not do. Self-control, I thought, was simply the procedure by which I made sure I followed the pattern.

I've come to believe now that self-control, in the spiritual sense, is almost the opposite of self-reliance. It is, rather, the quality which allows me, under threatening circumstances, to turn to another Source. That Source is usually found in prayer, the Bible, and the affirming support of friends. One of the outstanding examples of self-control in the Bible is the temptation of Jesus. Satan has Him alone, in a weakened condition in the desert. He offers Jesus jeweled dreams of power and recognition. If He had been self-reliant, Jesus would have accepted Satan's offers, for Satan appealed to His independence. He wanted Jesus to stand up against the Father and grab His own realm of authority. Jesus refused. He turned immediately to the Bible and drove off Satan's attack with blistering arguments from Scripture.

I used to think it was a sign of weakness to say, "I need help." I've come to believe the ability to say that should be one of the distinctions of the Christian. In the ballet *Salome*, Herod's stepdaughter Salome tries to entice John the Baptist. She ties him to a post and begins a sensuous dance in front of him. John's response is to close his eyes and cry out in prayer to God. He knew that the situation was too strong for him, so he cried out for help and cast the temptation aside. To me, that's self-control.

I like to tie this passage about the fruit of the Spirit, Galatians 5:22, to Jesus' metaphor in John 15:5: "Yes, I am the Vine and you are the branches. Whoever lives [or abides] in me and I in him shall produce a large crop of fruit.

For apart from me you can't do a thing." Self-control in my life is when I tenaciously, deliberately cling to Christ as the source. I turn to Him when temptation comes. I turn to Him for guidance and for daily strength.

Sometimes the Christian life is extremely lonely. Because I am in the public eye, I often get embroiled in controversy. Some group may be blessed by something I have said; another group may be extremely offended. God's process of growth for me has been to exercise my self-control, turn to Him, and cry, "Help!" When I do that, somehow, often in unexpected ways, He meets me.

12

Christ's Body

. . . I will build my church; and the gates of hell shall not prevail against it.

Matthew 16:18 KJV

When I was a kid I used to study insects and frogs and turtles and try to decide how I would have made them different if I had been God. Would I have put a hard shell on the back of the frog, so that he'd make a giant splash every time he jumped off a lily pad? Would I have given a dragonfly rotary wings instead of ones which go back and forth, so it would look like a helicopter? Would I have put an escape hatch at the top of the turtle's shell, like an army tank?

Believe me, I've grown to be very grateful that God, and

not Jay Kesler, created the world. But sometimes even now I fantasize what I would have made different. For example, sometimes I wish God would have made the soul visible. It could be a little organ inside the eye or somewhere that would grow and mature spiritually as the body grows physically.

A visible soul would solve several problems. It would dispel for all times arguments against the existence of the soul—any fool could plainly see it. But, even more important, it would easily demonstrate the concept of process that I've been discussing in this book.

Think of it. Everyone would be born with a tiny, shapeless soul. In some it would actually shrink, as people turned their backs on God. But when conversion came, and a person entered God's Kingdom, suddenly the miracle of birth would flash inside the person. That formless blob would take shape—an infant at first. Then we could watch the new Christian as God begins to work.

I think back over my Christian experience. What would it have been like to be able to *see* myself grow? I could look in a mirror at my visible soul and see the stunting of growth that occurred when I got all wrapped up in legalism or some blind prejudices. I could see spurts of growth as I learned to devote more time to God and lean on people with new honesty. When I finally decided that Christianity wasn't a set of exercises I could master and was a lifetime process of growth, I'm sure my visible soul would have zoomed through its puberty stages.

I'm fantasizing, of course. Yet, sometimes I have to stop and tell myself, "Jay, those enthusiastic new Christians who are so turned on and who are falling for all the traps you fell for—they're just babies. Give them time to grow!"

Time to grow. Acceptance of differences. A commitment to process. Those are the concepts I want to infuse into the Body of Christ. It's not been enough to work those things through on my own. I've had to grow to the point where I've said, "I need help. I need a family in which to grow spiritually, just as I grew up in a physical family."

The church is God's family, the environment for continuing growth. Many times it has been a terrible reflection on Christ's Body; the scars of the Inquisition and religious wars prove that. Yet Christ Himself predicted turmoil and faultiness in the first chapters of Revelation. I've come to appreciate the church as the environment where the Kingdom of God has got to happen. The best thing I've done in the past few years is to immerse myself in a small local church in Geneva, Illinois.

Yes, I believe in individual conversion, and changes in society worked through the efforts of individuals. But as I read the New Testament, I am impressed with the importance God seemed to place on the unwieldly group called the church. If I am committed to God's process, if I hope to have growing places in Him, I think it will happen most naturally in the protection of His Body.

What is the church, and what is it meant to be? Kids are always complaining to me about the church: it's old-fashioned, it's irrelevant, it's narrow-minded. Is the church meant to be perfect, constantly enjoyable, never grating? I don't believe so.

In my view, the church should not be a homogenous group. People shouldn't all have the same age, the same political views, the same income, the same skin color, the same politics or the same basic approach to life. The church is a mixture of the very young and the very old, the tolerant and the intolerant, the educated and the uneducated, the laboring man and the executive, the housewife and the professional woman.

I see the church's job as being a process like making ball bearings. To make ball bearings, take several fairly rough pieces of metal, and put them in a centerless grinder. Then

(*Hans Moser.*)

add an abrasive, such as, diamond dust or Carborundum, and a lot of oil. Spin the grinder at tremendous speed. As the oil moves the contents around, metal grates against metal and abrasive. Somehow in the midst of that process, those little pieces of metal are transformed into perfect, bright ball bearings.

The church is the same way. Mix together the young and the old, the wise and the ignorant. And if you deal with the real implications of Christ's message in issues such as, family, sex, jobs, worship, and money, you are going to wear on each other. The love of God is the oil—it makes it possible for the surfaces to wear on each other without burning each other up. Everything spins around, and we're able to rub the rough edges off each other.

Does that sound idealistic? Well, it is. The Kingdom of

God is a phenomenally revolutionary idea, and it will only work as we submit ourselves together to Christ as Lord of our lives, and allow His Spirit to lead us toward maturity. On the other hand, the church is probably the only institution in our society which has a chance to do this. The concept of the church is one of the most exciting concepts. Too much of the struggle of my Christian process has come when I've tried to go it alone, figuring out what God wants and attracting a following who believes likewise. I'm now learning that my process of growth is rather imbalanced if it does not occur within the Body of Christ.

Almost every other group in society is tied to productivity in some way, and those who can't keep pace and contribute get shunted aside. The old are forced to retire. The weak get fired. The ugly get socially ostracized. The young aren't listened to. If you can't produce, you're not valuable, and your opinions don't matter.

But the church, the Body of Christ, can be different. There's no product involved. Nobody has to be able to work so many hours or put out so much "product." As an extended family, it's the one place where both young and old, mentally retarded and gifted, ugly and beautiful—everyone—is valuable. Our worth is based on our existence as a creation of God, and our community is based on our common commitment to the Creator.

Where will I be ten years from now? Who knows! One thing is for sure: I'll be different from what I am today. My life in Christ is an adventure full of hairpin curves and screeching descents and smooth climbs. It's taken me a long time, but I've learned to accept that as God's style—His process—in making me more in Christ's image. And I've committed myself to letting Him work out that process within the fellowship of His Body.

I offer these experiences from my life. I'm sure they do not all fit your situation and you will not agree with all of my conclusions. I simply share these with you with the hope that not everyone will have to touch every stove to see if it is hot. But if you do, I encourage you with my experience. "He will never leave you nor forsake you" (*see* Hebrews 13:5).

What a wonderful God we have—he is the Father of our Lord Jesus Christ, the source of every mercy, and the one who so wonderfully comforts and strengthens us in our hardships and trials. And why does he do this? So that when others are troubled, needing our sympathy and encouragement, we can pass on to them this same help and comfort God has given us. You can be sure that the more we undergo sufferings for Christ, the more he will shower us with his comfort and encouragement.

2 Corinthians 1:4, 5

Bibliography

Board, Steve. "Editorial." *His,* May 1974, p. 32.

Buck, Pearl S. *The Good Earth.* New York: Grosset and Dunlap, 1931.

Bready, J. Wesley. "Eighteenth Century England: This Freedom—Whence?" In *The Cambridge Modern History.* New York: Cambridge University Press, 1970.

Bustanoby, Andre. "The Pastor and the Other Woman." *Christianity Today,* 30 August 1974, p.7.

Dillard, Annie. *Pilgrim at Tinker Creek.* New York: Harper Magazine Press, 1974.

Farrell, Frank E. "Unto One of the Least of These . . . ." *World Vision,* September 1972, p. 2.

Gergen, Kenneth J. "The Healthy, Happy Human Being Wears Many Masks." *Psychology Today,* May 1972, p. 31.

Golding, William. *Lord of the Flies.* New York: Capricorn Books, 1959.

Hatfield, Mark O. *Between a Rock and a Hard Place.* Waco, Texas: Word Books, 1976.

Howard, Thomas. "On Brazen Heavens." *Christianity Today,* 7 December 1973, pp. 8–11.

Lewis, C. S. *Prince Caspian.* New York: Macmillan, 1951.

—— *The Problem of Pain.* New York: Macmillan, 1962.

—— *The Weight of Glory and Other Addresses.* Grand Rapids: William B. Eerdmans, 1949, 1960.

MacDonald, George. *Life Essential: The Hope of the Gospel.* Edited by Rolland Hein. Wheaton, Illinois: Harold Shaw, 1974.

Miller, Keith. *The Taste of New Wine.* Waco, Texas: Word Books, 1965.

Muggeridge, Malcolm. *Jesus Rediscovered.* Wheaton, Illinois: Tyndale House, 1969.

Olsson, Karl. "The Hidden Dictator." *Faith at Work,* March 1972, p. 26.

Packer, J. I. *Evangelism and the Sovereignty of God.* Downers Grove, Illinois: Inter-Varsity, 1961.

Phillips, J. B. *New Testament Christianity.* London: Hodder and Stoughton, 1956.

Sartre, Jean-Paul. *No Exit and Three Other Plays.* New York: Random House, 1947.

Sayers, Dorothy L. *Christian Letters to a Post-Christian World.* Grand Rapids: William B. Eerdmans, 1969.

Smith, Margaret C. and Jeffers, Paul. *Gallant Women.* New York: McGraw-Hill, 1968.

Strommen, Merton P. *Five Cries of Youth.* New York: Harper and Row, 1974.

ten Boom, Corrie, and Sherrill, John and Elizabeth. *The Hiding Place.* Old Tappan, New Jersey: Fleming H. Revell, 1971.

Thielicke, Helmut. *Encounter With Spurgeon.* Philadelphia: Fortress Press, 1963.